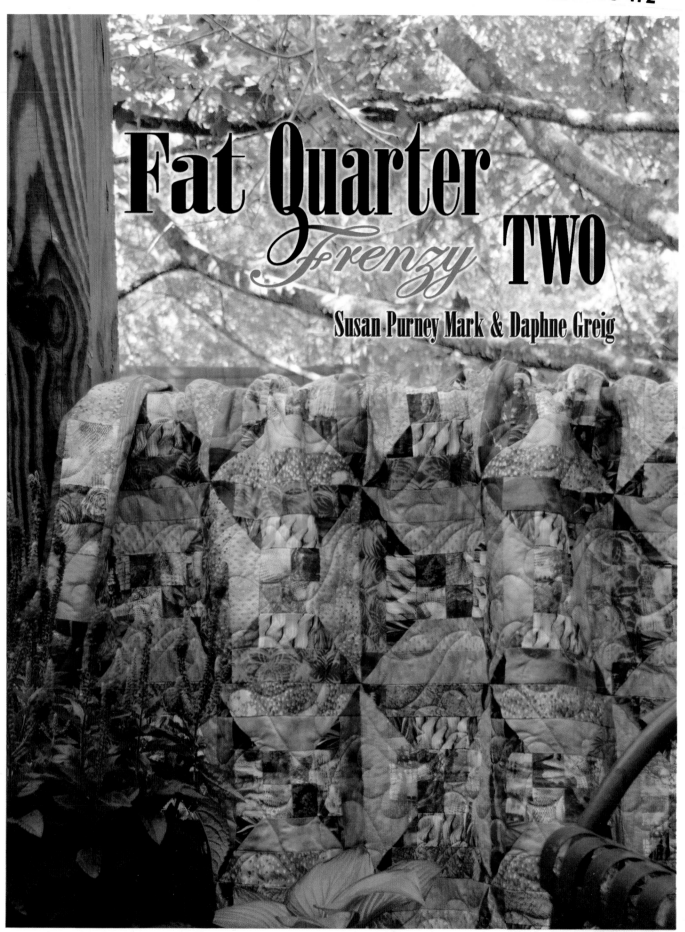

Fat Quarter
Frenzy TWO

Susan Purney Mark & Daphne Greig

Located in Paducah, Kentucky, the American Quilter's Society (AQS) is dedicated to promoting the accomplishments of today's quilters. Through its publications and events, AQS strives to honor today's quiltmakers and their work and to inspire future creativity and innovation in quiltmaking.

Executive Editor: Nicole Chambers
Editors: Linda Baxter Lasco & Barbara Smith
Graphic Design: Lynda Smith
Cover Design: Michael Buckingham
Photography: Charles R. Lynch

Library of Congress Cataloging-in-Publication Data

Mark, Susan Purney.
 Fat quarter frenzy two / by Susan Purney Mark & Daphne Greig.
   p. cm.
 ISBN 978-1-57432-948-3
 1. Patchwork--Patterns. 2. Quilting--Patterns. I. Greig, Daphne. II. Title.

 TT835.M27232 2008
 746.46'041--dc22

                        2007047710

Special thanks to Paul & Tina Baker of The Guild, LLC, Paducah, Kentucky, for generously sharing their fat quarter stash to grace these pages.

Additional copies of this book may be ordered from the American Quilter's Society, PO Box 3290, Paducah, KY 42002-3290, or online at: www.AmericanQuilter.com.

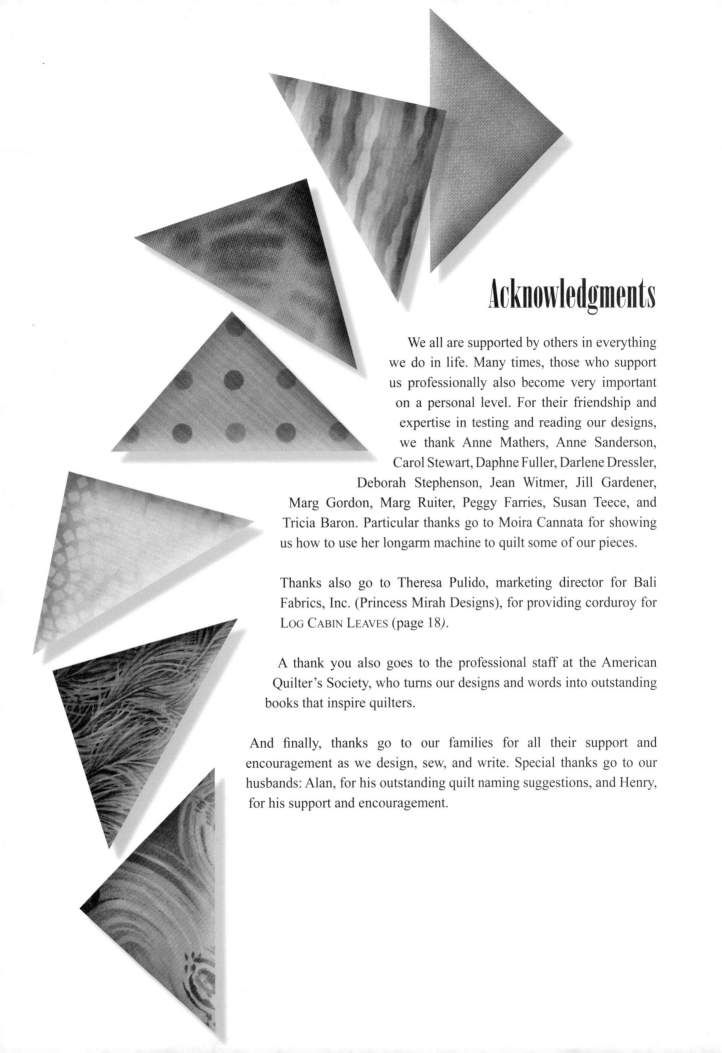

Acknowledgments

We all are supported by others in everything we do in life. Many times, those who support us professionally also become very important on a personal level. For their friendship and expertise in testing and reading our designs, we thank Anne Mathers, Anne Sanderson, Carol Stewart, Daphne Fuller, Darlene Dressler, Deborah Stephenson, Jean Witmer, Jill Gardener, Marg Gordon, Marg Ruiter, Peggy Farries, Susan Teece, and Tricia Baron. Particular thanks go to Moira Cannata for showing us how to use her longarm machine to quilt some of our pieces.

Thanks also go to Theresa Pulido, marketing director for Bali Fabrics, Inc. (Princess Mirah Designs), for providing corduroy for LOG CABIN LEAVES (page 18).

A thank you also goes to the professional staff at the American Quilter's Society, who turns our designs and words into outstanding books that inspire quilters.

And finally, thanks go to our families for all their support and encouragement as we design, sew, and write. Special thanks go to our husbands: Alan, for his outstanding quilt naming suggestions, and Henry, for his support and encouragement.

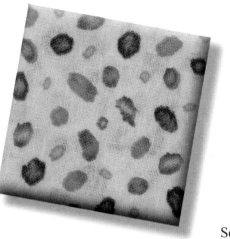

Contents

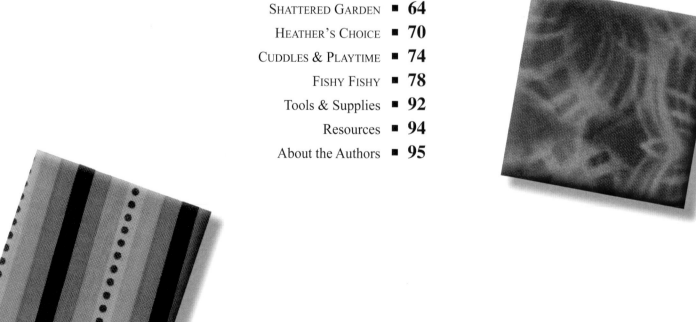

General Instructions

Quilters are creative and resourceful people. They can find something to make with even the smallest bits of fabric. As quilters, we are inspired by color and pattern and all the wonderful things we find in our local quilt shops. Some of the most inspiring things to be found are fat quarters. They are relatively inexpensive, about the cost of a latte, but they last longer and are non-fattening! They are our little treats in a busy world.

Who can resist that tempting stack of coordinated fabrics wrapped up in ribbons or folded in such ingenious ways? Quilters are visual people, and the attractive displays of fabrics and quilts in a shop will surely tempt us to buy.

Why Use Fat Quarters?

Do you know what a fat quarter is? Despite what your friends say, it is *not* a body part. It is a piece of fabric cut in a way that makes it more useable for quilters. A regular quarter yard of fabric measures 9" x 44". A fat quarter measures about 18" x approximately 22". It has the same number of square inches, but you can cut pieces wider than 9" from a fat quarter that you can't cut from a regular quarter yard.

If we need only a bit of fabric for a project, fat quarters provide an inexpensive solution and it is easy to pick up a couple each time we visit a quilt shop. By purchasing regularly, we can build a stash of fat quarters just as we do with regular cut yardage.

Building Your Stash

Just as we need the basics in cooking or in sewing clothing, we need a good foundation in our fabric inventory. In our kitchen pantry, we have quantities of flour and sugar for baking, and smaller quantities of specialty flours and sugars (rice flour, corn flour, brown sugar, icing sugar). In our quilting "pantry," we have yardage for borders and backgrounds and smaller amounts of fabric for our blocks and appliqué. Fat quarters can enable us to have a pantry full of ingredients for our quilts.

Tips for Buying Fat Quarters

■ Always be familiar with your stash so you know where there are missing colors, patterns, or themes. In our studio, we reorganize our fabrics at least once each year so we can see where we might need to add colors or styles. It is like meeting old friends, and we can see the fabric colors and patterns in a whole new light.

■ Be willing to pick up just the basics (tone-on-tone prints in all colors) and neutrals (beige, white, taupe, and cream). Neutrals are the building blocks of our quilts. They play a major supporting role in our designs.

■ When shopping, plan to buy a wide range of designs in each color to provide more choices for your quilts.

■ Stock up when stores have fat-quarter sales. This is a great time to build your inventory.

■ Watch for the new fabric introductions at your favorite quilt shop. It is always fun to have the newest fabrics in your stash.

■ Visit quilt shops outside your area when you are on vacation. A few fat quarters make great mementos of the special places you have visited. Why not make a memory quilt with the fat quarters you bought during your vacation? This would be a perfect time to use some vacation photos printed on fabric as well.

■ When buying your fabric, it is important to look at color, value (light to dark), theme (country, floral, ethnic, etc.), and scale (large or small print).

You will need a range of values and scales for your fat quarter quilts. We tend to buy fabrics that are medium in value but it is important to have a range of values to choose from. Select the themes that you like to work with.

- Often, fabric companies will have the same print in a wide range of colors and values. This is a great opportunity to add to your collection.

Selecting Fabric for the Projects

Many of the projects have been tested by our friends. They chose their favorite fabrics for their quilt projects and so can you. Look at the photo of your chosen quilt and consider how you can substitute fabrics that excite you.

Here are some of the ways we selected fabrics for our projects: ASIAN FLIGHT, page 42, was designed to showcase a large-scale print, whose design would be lost if cut into smaller squares.

For CUDDLES AND PLAYTIME, page 74, a line of tone-on-tone colors shaded from a light value through a medium value was used.

Some projects contain a repeated block, for example SPRINGTIME RAMBLER, page 28. To maintain the coordinated look for this quilt, we chose the same colors for the two different blocks, but placed them differently.

Do you collect a specific type of fabric? Coordinated collections of fat quarters may be just the thing for your chosen project. Consider selecting fabrics with a common theme or mood. You could also select a special fabric for the border of your quilt, then have fun seeing how many coordinating fabrics you can use for the blocks.

Care and Feeding of Fat Quarters

We recommend prewashing your fabrics before using them. It is easiest to do this as soon as you bring them home from the store so they will go into your storage area ready to be used. We like to use the mesh lingerie bags for washing these small amounts of fabric.

Sort the fabrics by color, just as you do your regular laundry. Put like colors together and wash them on a gentle cycle in your washing machine. Remove the fat quarters from the mesh bag and place them in your dryer on a low heat setting. Remove them from the dryer when they are damp dry and press dry with an iron. Be sure the fabrics are completely dry before folding them for storage. With the mesh bag method, you can put the fat quarters in with your regular laundry.

We test the darkest colors for colorfastness by washing them separately in a small sink rather than putting them through the washer.

There are many ways to store your fat quarters. Some people like to keep them separate from their yardage; others store by color or theme. We tend to store the packs of fat quarters separately until we determine what we'll use them for. We like to keep single fat quarters sorted by color and separate from our regular stash. It is up to you to decide what works best. But remember that humidity and light are your fabric's worst enemies, so keep fabrics dry and out of direct light whenever possible.

We all know that colors and styles go in and out of fashion, so don't save the good stuff. Use it up. There will be more to tempt you in the future.

Playtime with Fat Quarters

Get more from your stash! If you and your quilting friends have larger fabric pieces (a half yard or more), and you can't even remember why you bought them, why not cut them into fat quarters and have a trading session?

If you have fabrics you know you won't use, cut them into fat quarters and have a fundraiser for your guild. Donate the fat quarters to a sale table and set the same price for each fat quarter.

Many quilt guilds are involved with some form of an exchange among their members. Many of them take part in what is often called "tinners" because the fabrics are stored in cookie tins. Here is how it works:

Each member chooses a theme and brings a cookie tin containing one fat quarter. The theme could be birds, houses, flowers—you get the idea. Participants exchange tins at the monthly guild meeting, make a block using the theme as inspiration, and add a fat quarter to the tin. They hand the tin

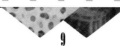
back at the next meeting, and the tins are exchanged again. This process is repeated each month for as many months as desired. At the end, the participants have a variety of blocks relating to their themes and a lot of fat quarters for their quilts.

Keeping Track

We have found the use of a swatch chart to be invaluable for keeping track of the fabrics and their placement in our quilts. The swatch chart serves a number of functions. First, it can help you remember which fabrics go in certain places. For example, if you are following instructions that refer to fabric A, B, or C or light, medium light, or dark, it is not always easy to remember which is which by just looking. When there are several fat quarters required for certain colors or prints, as in STRIP DOODLES on page 58, a swatch chart is invaluable. It is a great reference when deciding on fabric placement.

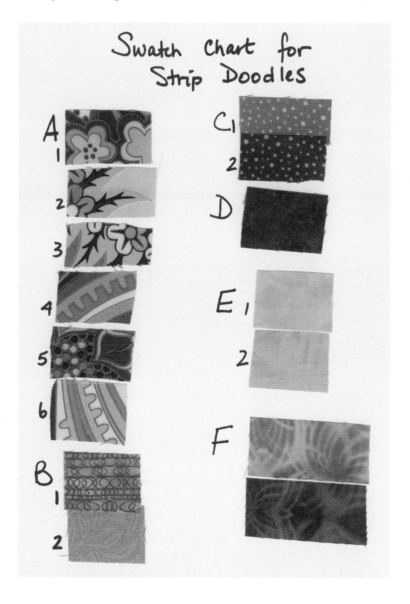

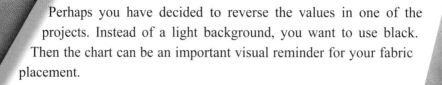
Perhaps you have decided to reverse the values in one of the projects. Instead of a light background, you want to use black. Then the chart can be an important visual reminder for your fabric placement.

A swatch chart is a useful tool for your quilting and design work. You can create your own for any of the projects. Simply list the fat quarters and yardage given for each project and tape or glue a small swatch of fabric beside the list. You can also leave space for any notes that you might want to add to help in making your quilt. We also recommend placing cut pieces into zipper-top bags to keep them organized.

Using Yardage

We love the opportunity that fat quarters offer in variety and choice, but all the projects are suitable for yardage as well. It is simple to substitute yardage by adding up the number of fat quarters for each color or value and dividing by four. (Four fat quarters equal one yard.) So if the project requires six light fat quarters, you will need 1½ yards of light fabric.

Some of the designs are suitable for substituting scraps for the fat quarters. Read fabric requirements carefully to make sure you have enough fabric.

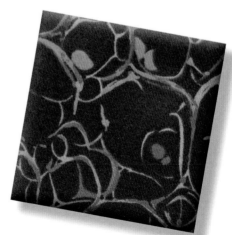

Displaying Your Quilts

You may want to display your wall- or medium-sized quilts by hanging them on a wall. We suggest you sew a fabric sleeve to the back of your quilt and use a metal or wood rod to hang the quilt. The rod will support the weight of the project evenly. Here are our instructions for making a hanging sleeve:

Cut a piece of muslin (or extra backing fabric) that measures 6" wide by the width of the quilt.

Finish the two short edges by folding ¼" to the wrong side twice and sewing along the edges.

Fold the strip in half along its length, wrong sides together, and sew the long raw edges with a ½" seam allowance.

Press the seam allowance open. Flatten the tube and center the seam on the back of the sleeve.

Pin the sleeve to the quilt back, just below the binding at the top edge, centering it across the width. Slip-stitch the top edge of the sleeve in place by hand.

Push the bottom edge of the tube up a bit (to allow space for the rod) and pin the bottom edge in place. Again, slip-stitch the edge securely, being careful that your stitches do not show on the front of the quilt.

Insert your rod inside the tube so it doesn't touch the back of the quilt. Hang the rod on brackets or nails securely fastened to your wall.

If your quilt is more than 48" wide, you may need to add additional support in the center or at intervals. In this case, the hanging sleeve could be made in two or more sections. Allow space between the sections for additional brackets.

Tropical Punch

Finished quilt: 51½" x 69½" ↶ Finished block: 9" x 9"

Daphne chose bright, punchy colors for this quilt with medium and dark values of coral, raspberry, orange, and bright green. Accents of purple, blue, and a hint of yellow tie all these strong colors together. This quilt would be equally effective with soft pastels. Black-and-white prints would make a very bold statement.

Fabric Requirements

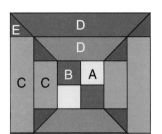

Fabric A (yellow)	1 fat quarter
Fabric B (purple)	1 fat quarter
Fabric C (mixed greens)	6 fat quarters
Fabric D (reds, pinks, & oranges)	8 fat quarters
Fabric E (mixed blues)	4 fat quarters
Inner border (dark)	1 fat quarter
Backing	3½ yards
Binding	½ yard
Batting	58" x 76"

Cutting Instructions

Fabric A—*cut from the **long** side*
1 strip 3" wide, cut into 4 rectangles 3" x 3½" and 1 rectangle 3" x 4¼"
7 strips 2"

Fabric B—*cut from the **long** side*
1 strip 3" wide, cut into 4 rectangles 3" x 3½" and 1 rectangle 3" x 4¼"
7 strips 2" wide

Fabric C—*cut from the **long** side*
*from **two** fat quarters cut* – 7 strips 2" wide, cut into 35 rectangles 2" x 3½" (total of 70)
*from **three** fat quarters* – 8 strips 2" wide, cut into 24 rectangles 2" x 6½" (total of 70)
*from **one** fat quarter* – 5 strips 3" wide, cut into 4 squares and 20 rectangles 3" x 3½"

Fabric D—*cut from the **long** side*
*from **three** fat quarters cut* – 8 strips 2" wide, cut into 24 rectangles 2" x 6½" (total of 70)
*from **five** fat quarters cut* – 1 strip 3" wide, cut into 4 rectangles 3" x 3½" (total of 20)
          and 1 rectangle 3" x 4¼" (total of 5)
7 strips 2" wide, cut into 14 rectangles 2" x 9½" (total of 70)

Cutting Instructions (cont.)

- **Fabric E**—*cut from the long side*
    1 strip 3" wide, cut into 4 rectangles 3" x 3½" (total of 16) and
            1 rectangle 3" x 4¼" (total of 4)
    7 strips 2" wide, cut into 70 squares (total of 280)

- **Inner border**—*cut from the short side*
    14 strips 1½" wide

Making the blocks

Sew the A and B strips together to make 7 strip-sets. Press seam allowances toward the dark strips. From the strip-sets, cut 70 segments 2" wide.

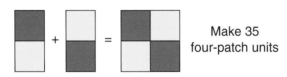

Cut 70   Make 7 strip-sets

Make 35 four-patch units.

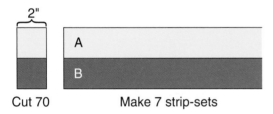

Make 35
four-patch units

Sew matching 2" x 3½" C rectangles to opposite sides of the four-patch units as shown. Pay attention to the position of the light and dark squares in the four-patch.

Draw a diagonal line on the back of the E squares. Place over the end of a 2" x 6½" D rectangle, right sides together. Sew on the drawn line.

Flip the E square back along the sewn line and press from the right side. Trim the two underlayers as shown, leaving a ¼" seam allowance.

Repeat at the other end of the rectangle, paying attention to the direction of the drawn diagonal line. Flip, press, and trim as before.

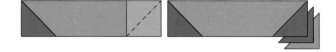

Sew matching D/E units to opposite sides of the four-patch units as shown.

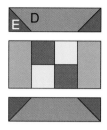

Sew matching 2" x 6½" C rectangles to opposite sides of your growing block as shown.

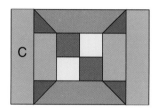

Sew E squares to the 2" x 9½" D rectangles to make the D/E units as shown. Press and trim as before.

Add matching D/E units to opposite sides of the block. Make 35.

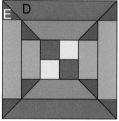

Make 35

Arrange the blocks in 5 rows of 7 blocks each, alternating the position of the greens in the blocks as shown. Join the blocks into rows, then join the rows.

Adding the borders

Sew the inner border strips end-to-end with diagonal seams to make one long strip. Measure the length of the quilt through the middle. From the long strip, cut 2 inner border strips that measurement. Sew the strips to the sides of the quilt and press seam allowances toward the border.

Measure the width of the quilt through the center, including the inner border strips, and cut 2 border strips that length. Sew them to the top and bottom of the quilt and press seam allowances toward the border.

Making the pieced border

Randomly select 19 rectangles 3" x 3½" and sew them together on the 3" sides to make one border strip. Add a 3" x 4½" rectangle to each end of the strip. Repeat to make a second strip and sew these to the sides of the quilt.

Side border – make 2

Randomly select 13 rectangles 3" x 3½" and sew them together on the 3" sides to make one strip. Add a 3" x 4½" rectangle and a 3" square to each end of the strip. Repeat to make a second strip and sew these to the top and bottom of the quilt.

Top and bottom border – make 2

Layer the quilt top with backing and batting then quilt by hand or machine. Cut the binding fabric into 2¼" wide strips to bind your quilt.

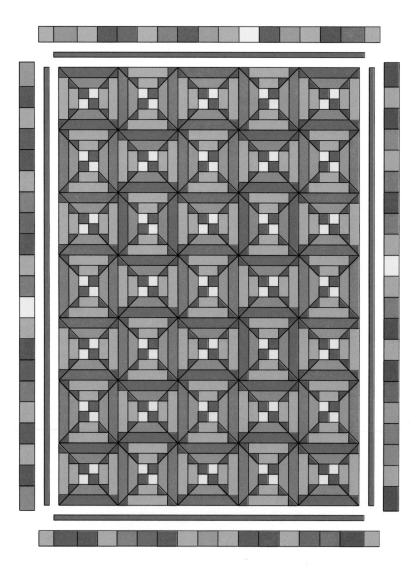

TROPICAL PUNCH, 51½" x 69½" • made by Daphne Greig

Log Cabin Leaves

Finished quilt: 54" x 66" ↶ Finished block: 12" x 12"

These leaves look as if they've just been blown off the tree. Combine an easy Nine-Patch leaf with Log Cabin strips to make the blocks. Look for leaf prints in shades of green, rust, and gold for a great fall quilt. Daphne used fine batik corduroy in her quilt. For corduroy, she recommends using a sharp 80/12 machine needle and pressing seam allowances open to reduce bulk.

Fabric Requirements

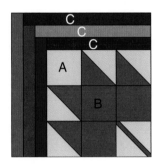

Fabric A (background–mixed light prints)	4 fat quarters
Fabric B (leaves–mixed prints)	5 fat quarters
Fabric C (logs and inner border–mixed prints)	8 fat quarters
Fabric D (outer border)	2 different fat quarters
Backing	3¾ yards
Binding	2 different fat quaters
Batting	60" x 72"

Cutting Instructions

▨ **Fabric A**—*cut from the long side*
  1 strip 3½" wide, cut into 5 squares (total of 20)
  3 strips 4" wide, cut into 15 squares (total of 60)

■ **Fabric B**—*cut from the short side.* These fat quarters must measure at least 21" long.
  3 strips 3½" wide, cut into 12 squares (total of 60)
  2 strips 4" wide, cut into 8 squares (total of 40)
  2 strips 1¼" wide, cut into 4 rectangles 1¼" x 5" (total of 20)

■ **Fabric C**—*cut from the long side*
  11 strips 1½" wide

■ **Fabric D**—*cut from the long side*
  6 strips 2½" wide

Making the blocks

Draw a diagonal line on the wrong side of 10 A 4" squares of each fabric (40 squares total).

Layer the marked A squares with B squares, right sides together. Sew ¼" on each side of the drawn line. Cut along the marked line and press the seam allowance toward the darker fabric. Trim to 3½" square. Make 80 half-square triangles.

Make 40
of each

Cut the remaining 20 A 4" squares on the diagonal to make 40 triangles.

Cut 20 squares

Join two matching A triangles with a B rectangle as shown. Press toward the rectangle. Trim to 3½" square.

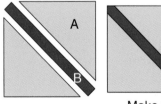

Make 20

Matching background and leaf fabrics, lay out the pieces for each block as shown. Join the squares in rows and join the rows. Press the seams open. The leaf blocks should measure 9½" square.

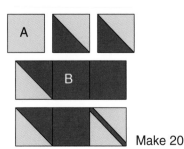

Make 20

Join all the same color log cabin strips together end-to-end, to make a continuous strip of each color. Press seam allowances open.

Sort the leaf blocks into 4 groups with 5 different blocks in each group. Select one group of blocks and 6 different log cabin strips.

Chain-sew one group of blocks to a log cabin strip, positioning the blocks as shown. Press the strip away from the blocks. Cut the blocks apart and trim the strip even with the edges of each leaf block.

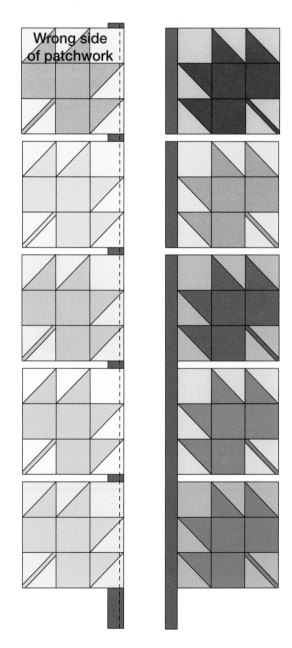

Wrong side of patchwork

In the same manner, add a different colored strip to the adjacent side of the 5 blocks, as shown, again paying attention to the orientation of the blocks.

Repeat these steps until you have added 3 log cabin strips to the 2 sides of each block, using a different colored strip each time. The blocks should measure 12½" square. Label these blocks #1.

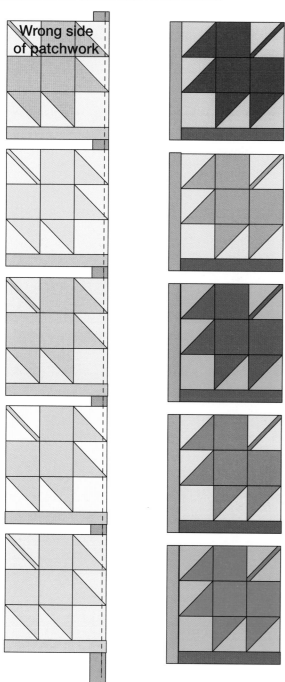

Block #1
Make 5

Working with another group of 5 blocks and 6 different log cabin strips, sew strips to 2 different adjacent sides as shown to make five of block #2.

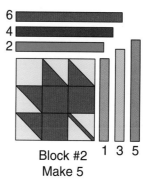

Block #2
Make 5

Continue in the same manner to make blocks #3 and #4, adding the log cabin strips to different adjacent sides as shown.

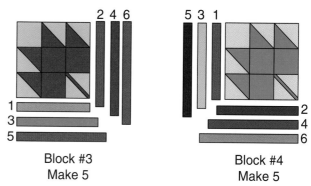

Block #3
Make 5

Block #4
Make 5

Arrange the blocks in 5 rows of 4 blocks each, as shown. Sew the blocks in rows, then join the rows. Press seams open.

Adding the borders

For the inner border, join the remaining log cabin strips end-to-end to make one long strip. Press seam allowances open.

Measure the length of the quilt through the center and cut 2 inner border pieces that measurement from the long strip. Sew them to the sides of the quilt. Press the seam allowances toward the border.

Measure the width of the quilt through the center and cut 2 inner border pieces that measurement from the long strip. Sew these to the top and bottom. Press the seam allowances toward the border.

Join the outer border strips from one fat quarter end-to-end. Join the outer border strips from the second fat quarter end-to-end.

Measure the length of the quilt through the center and cut a piece that measurement from each of the outer border strips. Sew them to the sides of the quilt. Press the seam allowances toward the border.

Measure the width of the quilt through the center and cut a piece that measurement from each of the outer border strips. Sew them to the top and bottom of the quilt.

Layer the quilt top with the backing and batting then quilt the layers by hand or machine.

Daphne layered her quilt with fleece and no batting. She quilted the layers with an all-over meandering design.

From the long side of each binding fat quarter, cut 7 strips 2¼" wide. Join the strips with diagonal seams and use your favorite method to bind the raw edges of your quilts.

LOG CABIN LEAVES, 54" x 66" • made by Daphne Greig

Raspberry Ripple

Finished quilt: 64" x 82" ↶ Finished block: 9" x 9"

Make this lap quilt in flannels and it's sure to keep someone warm and cozy all through a long cold winter. Or choose bright batiks for a college student, for a bright sunny reminder of home.

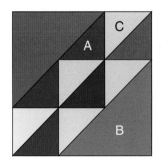

Fabric Requirements

Fabric A (light prints)	6 different fat quarters
Fabric B (medium prints)	8 different fat quarters
Fabric C (dark prints)	6 different fat quarters
Border and binding	2 yards
Backing	5¼ yards
Batting	70" x 88"

Cutting Instructions

Fabrics A & C—*cut from the **long** side*

4 strips 3⅞" wide, cut into 20 squares (total of 120 each light and dark squares)

Fabric B—*Note:* These fat quarters must measure at least 20 ⅝" long.

2 strips 6⅞", cut into 6 squares (total of 48)

Making the blocks

Draw a diagonal line on the wrong sides of 72 A squares. Layer the A squares right sides together with the C squares.

72 = 144

Sew ¼" on each side of the drawn line. Cut along the line and press the seam allowances toward C. If necessary, trim the units to 3½". You will have 144 half-square triangles.

Cut 48 A, B, and C squares in half diagonally to make 96 triangles of each.

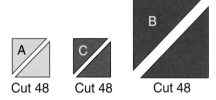

Add an A triangle to 48 half-square triangles as shown.

Add an A and C triangle to opposite sides of 48 half-square triangles as shown.

Add a C triangle to 48 half-square triangles as shown.

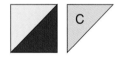

Join one of each of these units to form the center unit of the blocks.

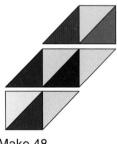

Make 48

Add a B triangle to both sides of the center units. Press the seams toward the B triangles.

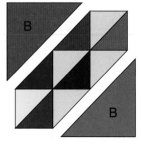

Make 48

Arrange the blocks in rows of 6 blocks each as shown.

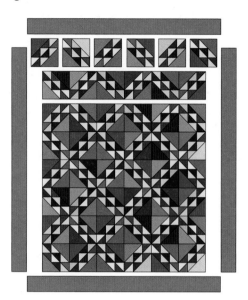

Sew the blocks together in rows then sew the rows together. Press all seam allowances open for a flatter quilt, if desired.

Adding the borders

From the border fabric, cut 8 strips 5½" wide, selvage to selvage. Sew these strips together, end-to-end with diagonal seams, to make one long strip.

Measure the length of the quilt through the center and cut 2 border pieces that measurement from the long strip. Sew them to the sides of the quilt. Press the seam allowances toward the border.

Measure the width of the quilt through the center and cut 2 pieces that measurement from the long strip. Sew these to the top and bottom. Press the seam allowances toward the border.

Layer the quilt top with the backing and batting then quilt the layers by hand or machine.

Susan quilted a loopy floral design over the center part of the quilt and repeated a similar design for the border.

From the binding fabric, cut 8 strips 2¼" wide, selvage to selvage. Use these strips and your favorite method to bind the raw edges of your quilt.

RASPBERRY RIPPLE, 64" x 82", made by Susan Purney Mark

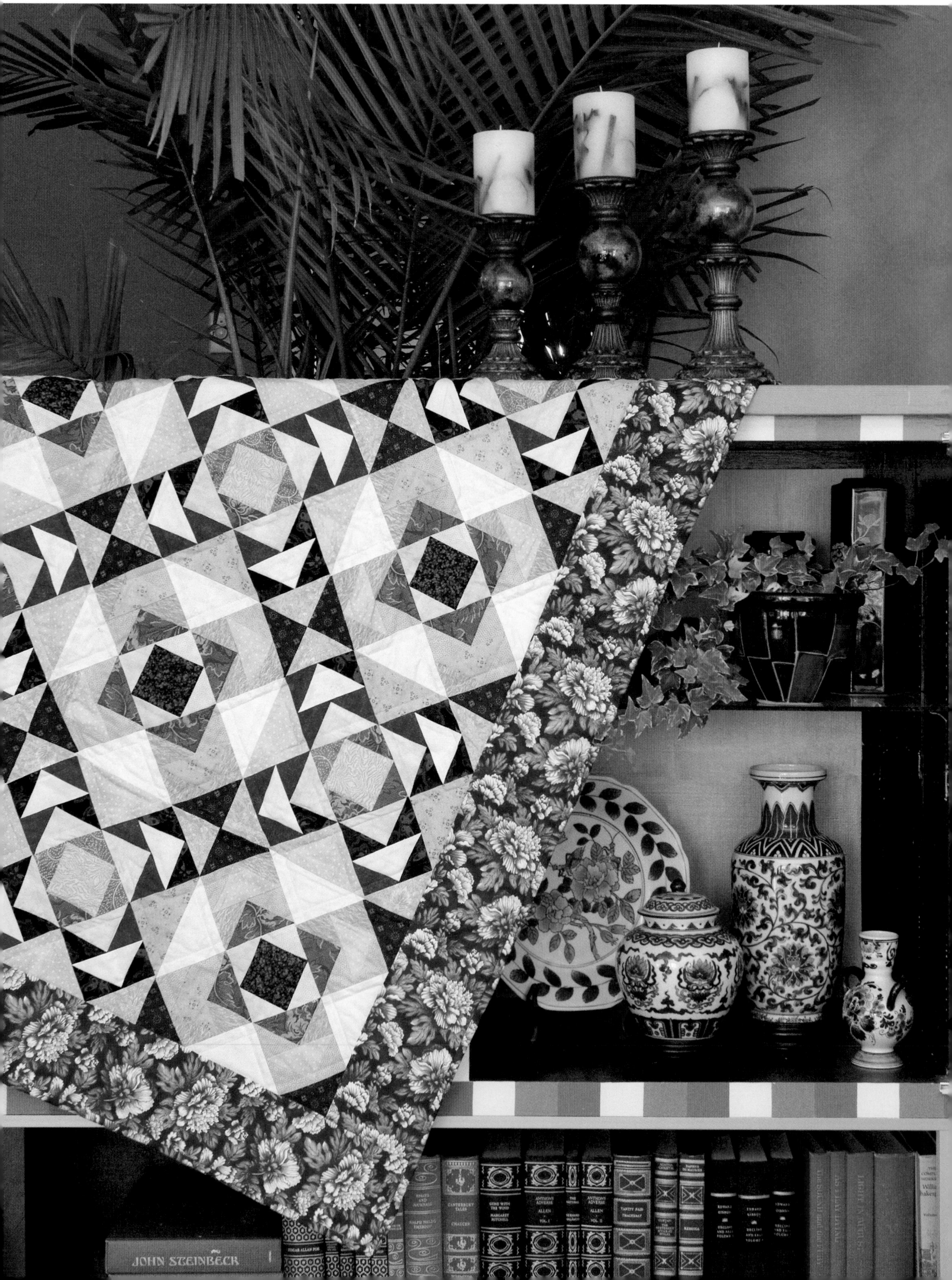
JOHN STEINBECK

Springtime Rambler

Finished quilt: 50" x 60" ↺ Finished block: 10" x 10"

Blue and yellow is a favorite color combination. There are so many fabric designs to choose from. By using different values of these colors, you will create a stunning lap quilt or wallhanging that has a surprising woven effect.

Fabric Requirements

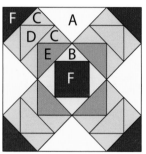

Block 1

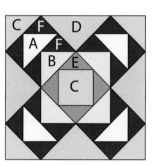

Block 2

Fabric A (light yellow)	3 fat quarters
Fabric B (medium yellow)	2 fat quarters
Fabric C (dark yellow)	4 fat quarters
Fabric D (light blue)	3 fat quarters
Fabric E (medium blue)	2 fat quarters
Fabric F (dark blue)	4 fat quarters
Border and binding	1¾ yards
Backing	3⅜ yards
Batting	56" x 66"

Cutting Instructions

Fabrics A & D—*cut from the **long** side*

*from **two** fat quarters of each color cut* – 4 strips 6¼" wide, cut into 10 squares (total of 20)

*from **one** fat quarter of each color cut* – 3 strips 4¾" wide, cut into 10 squares (total of 20)

Fabrics B & E—*cut from the **long** side*

*from **one** fat quarter of each color cut* – 3 strips 2⅝" wide, cut into 20 squares (total of 40)

*from **one** fat quarter of each color cut* – 3 strips 4¾" wide, cut into 10 squares (total of 20)

Fabrics C & F—*cut from the **long** side*

*from **two** fat quarters of each color cut* – 6 strips 2⅝" wide, cut into 80 squares (total of 160)

*from **one** fat quarter of each color cut* – 4 strips 3⅜" wide, cut into 20 squares (total of 40)

*from **one** fat quarter of each color cut* – 2 strips 3" wide, cut into 10 squares (total of 20)

For efficiency, you can layer 2 fat quarters together, one of each color, and cut both at the same time.

Making Block 1

To make flying geese units, first mark a diagonal line on the wrong side of 4 C 2⅝" squares. Lay 2 squares right sides together with a D 4¾" square as shown.

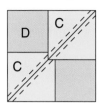

Sew ¼" on each side of the marked line. Cut along the marked line and press the small triangles away from the large triangles, making 2 units as shown.

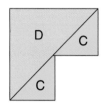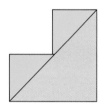

Place another C square right sides together on both units as shown and sew ¼" on each side of the marked line. Cut along the line and press the small triangles away from the large triangle.

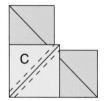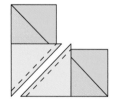

You now have 4 flying geese units. Repeat with the remaining C and D squares to make a total of 40 flying geese units.

Make 40

In the same manner, make 40 flying geese units from the C and E squares.

Make 40

Cut all the 2⅝" B squares in half diagonally to make 40 triangles. Repeat for the 3⅜" F squares. Cut all the 6¼" A squares twice on the diagonal.

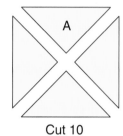

Cut 20   Cut 20   Cut 10

Make 10 square-in-a-square units with the B triangles and 3" F squares as shown.

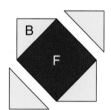

Make 10

Assemble block 1 as shown.

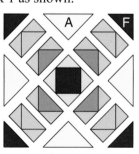

Make 10

Making Block 2

The construction sequence for block 2 is the same as for block 1. Make 40 flying geese units from the A and F squares and 40 units from the B and F squares.

Make 40   Make 40

Cut all the 2⅝" E squares in half diagonally to make 40 triangles. Repeat for the 3⅜" C squares. Cut all the 6¼" D squares twice on the diagonal.

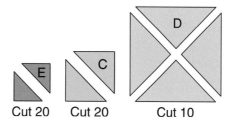

Cut 20   Cut 20   Cut 10

Make 10 square-in-a-square units with the E triangles and 3" C squares.

Make 10

Assemble block 2 as shown.

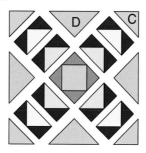

Make 10

Adding the borders

Arrange the blocks in 5 rows of 4 blocks each, alternating them in a checkerboard style. Sew the blocks in rows, then join the rows. Press seams open.

From the border fabric, cut 7 strips 5½" wide, selvage to selvage. Sew these strips together, end-to-end with diagonal seams, to make one long strip.

Measure the length of the quilt through the center and cut 2 border pieces that measurement from the long strip. Sew them to the sides of the quilt. Press the seam allowances toward the border.

Measure the width of the quilt through the center and cut 2 pieces that measurement from the long strip. Sew these to the top and bottom. Press the seam allowances toward the border.

Layer the quilt top with the backing and batting then quilt the layers by hand or machine.

Susan chose a diagonal design for the quilting and created a floral design for the border.

From the binding fabric, cut 7 strips 2¼" wide, selvage to selvage. Use these strips and your favorite method to bind the raw edges of your quilt.

SPRINGTIME RAMBLER, 50" x 60" • made by Susan Purney Mark

Amish Stars

Finished quilt: 72" x 72" ↶ Finished block: 12" x 12"

You do not need a focus fabric for this quilt design. Instead, this pattern provides a great way to use your collection of tone-on-tone or solid fat quarters in one quilt. Pay particular attention to the values (very light to very dark). For the sashing and cornerstones, select colors that contrast with the fat quarters used in the blocks.

Block 1

Block 2

Fabric Requirements
Block 1

Fabric A (background–very light)	5 fat quarters
Use 5 different fat quarters to vary the background of your blocks.	
Fabric B (light)	1 fat quarter
Fabric C (medium)	2 fat quarters
Fabric D (dark)	1 fat quarter
Fabric E (star points–very dark)	5 fat quarters
Use 5 different fat quarters to vary the star points of your blocks.	

Block 2

Fabric F (very light)	1 fat quarter
Fabric G (star points–light)	2 fat quarters
Use 2 different fat quarters to vary the star points of your blocks.	
Fabric H (medium)	1 fat quarter
Fabric I (background–medium dark)	4 fat quarters
Use 4 different fat quarters to vary the background of your blocks.	
Fabric J (dark)	1 fat quarter
Fabric K (very dark)	1 fat quarter
Fabric L (very light)	1 fat quarter
Sashing (assorted medium darks)	8 fat quarters
Cornerstones	1 fat quarter
Backing	4¾ yards
Binding	¾ yard
Batting	78" x 78"

Cutting Instructions

Block 1

Fabric A (very light–background)—*cut from the **long** side*
1 strip 6¼" wide, cut into 3 squares (total of 13)
4 strips 2½" wide, cut into 12 rectangles 2½" x 4" (total of 52) and
        12 rectangles 2½" x 2" (total of 52) *You only need 1 square 6¼" and 4 of
        each rectangle size from the fifth fat quarter.*

Fabric B (light)—*cut from the **long** side*
3 strips 3¼" wide, cut into 13 squares then trim the last strip to cut 2 squares
2⅜" x 2⅜"
3 strips 2⅜" wide, cut into 24 squares

Fabric C (medium)—*cut from the **long** side*
3 strips 2" wide, cut into 28 squares from one fat quarter's strips and 24 from
the other (total of 52)
4 strips 2" wide, cut into 28 rectangles 2" x 2½" from one fat quarter and 24
from the other (total of 52)

Fabric D (dark)—*cut from the **long** side*
4 strips 2⅜" wide, cut into 26 squares

Fabric E (very dark–star points)
52 star point templates
52 reversed star point templates
        *Cut star points and reversed star points in sets
        of 4 so the star points in each block will match.*

Block 2

Fabrics F & K (very light & very dark)—*cut from the **long** side*
10 strips 1½" wide (total 20 strips)

Fabric G (light–star points)—*cut from the **long** side*
2 strips 1½" wide (total of 4 strips)
4 strips 3⅜" wide, cut into 48 squares (total of 8 strips)

Fabric H (medium)—*cut from the **long** side*
8 strips 1½" wide

Cutting Instructions *(continued)*

■ **Fabric I** (medium dark background)—*cut from the **long** side*
   1 strip 6¼" wide, cut into 3 squares (total of 12)
   1 strip 3" wide, cut into 12 rectangles 1½" x 3" (total of 48)
   2 strips 4" wide, cut into 12 rectangles 3" x 4" (total of 48)

■ **Fabric J** (dark)—*cut from the **long** side*
   4 strips 1½" wide

□ **Fabric L** (very light–centers of blocks 1 & 2)—*cut from the **long** side*
   2 strips 2½" wide, cut into 13 squares (block 1 centers)
   3 strips 3½" wide, cut into 12 squares (block 2 centers)

Making Block 1

Mark a diagonal line on the wrong side of the 2⅜" B squares. Layer with the D squares, right sides together.

Sew ¼" on each side of the marked line. Cut along the line to make 2 half-square units. Press the seam allowance toward the darker triangle. If necessary, trim the units to 2". Make 52.

Make 52
half-square triangles

Join the half-square triangles with the matching C rectangles and the 2½" L squares to make 13 block 1 center units.

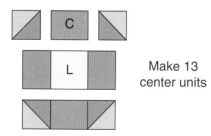

Make 13
center units

Cut the 6¼" A squares in quarters diagonally to make 52 triangles.

Cut the 3¼" B squares in quarters diagonally to make 52 triangles.

Make 52 star point units as shown, matching the colors of the star points and background fabrics in each unit.

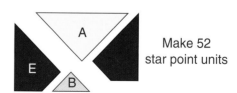

Make 52
star point units

Make 52 corner units as shown, matching the background fabrics in each unit.

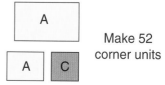

Make 52
corner units

Assemble block 1 as shown, matching the background and the colors of the C rectangles in the center units with the C squares in the corner units. Match the star point units within each block.

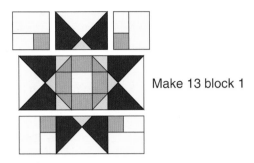

Make 13 block 1

Making Block 2

Sew pairs of F and K strips together to make 10 strip-sets. Press the seam allowance toward the darker strips. Cut into 48 segments 3½".

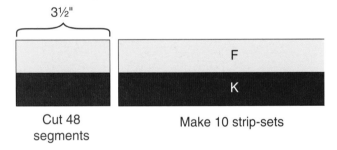

3½"

Cut 48 segments

Make 10 strip-sets

Sew pairs of G and H strips together to make 4 strip-sets. Press the seam allowance toward the darker strips. Cut 48 segments 1½" wide.

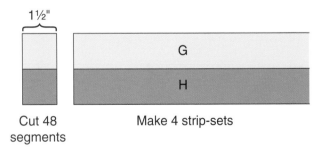

1½"

Cut 48 segments

Make 4 strip-sets

Sew pairs of H and J strips together to make 4 strip-sets. Press the seam allowance toward the darker strips. Cut 48 segments 1½" wide.

1½"

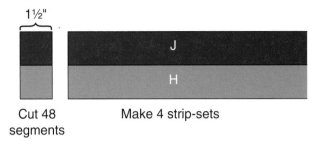

J

H

Cut 48 segments

Make 4 strip-sets

Join the G/H and H/J units to make 48 four-patch units, matching the H color in each unit.

Make 48 four-patch units

With these units and the 3½" L squares, make the block 2 center units. Use the matching four-patch units at the corners.

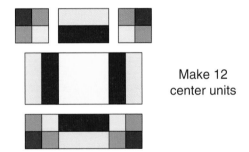

Make 12 center units

To make the flying geese units for the star points, first mark a diagonal line on the wrong side of 4 matching 3⅜" G squares.

Layer two G squares right sides together with one 6¼" I square as shown. Sew ¼" on each side of the marked line. Cut along the marked line and press the small triangles away from the large triangles to complete 2 units.

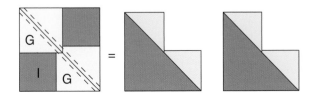

G

I   G

=

Place another G square on both of the units as shown, right sides together, and sew ¼" on each side of the marked line. Cut along the line and press the small triangles away from the large triangle. You now have 4 flying geese units.

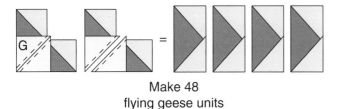

Make 48
flying geese units

Repeat with the remaining G and I squares to make 48 flying geese units.

Add a 1½" x 3" I rectangle to both ends of 24 flying geese units, matching the background color.

Make 24

Join the center units, matching flying geese units, and matching 3" x 4" I rectangles to make 12 block 2 as shown.

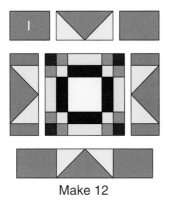

Make 12

Assembling the quilt

From the *short* side of the 8 sashing fat quarters, cut 8 strips 2½" wide from which you cut rectangles 2½" x 12½". You need 60 rectangles.

From the long side of the cornerstone fat quarter, cut 5 strips 2½" wide from which you cut 36 squares 2½" x 2½".

Arrange the blocks in an alternating pattern, with the sashing strips and cornerstones between the blocks and around the outside edges.

Sew 5 blocks and 6 vertical sashing strips together to make a block row. Make a total of 5 block rows. Sew 5 horizontal sashing strips and 6 cornerstones together to make a sashing row. Make 6 sashing rows. Then sew the block and sashing rows together.

Layer the quilt top with the backing and batting and quilt the layers by hand or machine.

Daphne hand quilted a grid design of double straight lines spaced ¼" apart. She quilted a simple diamond cable in the sashing.

From the binding fabric, cut 8 strips 2¼" wide, selvage to selvage. Use these strips and your favorite method to bind the raw edges of your quilt.

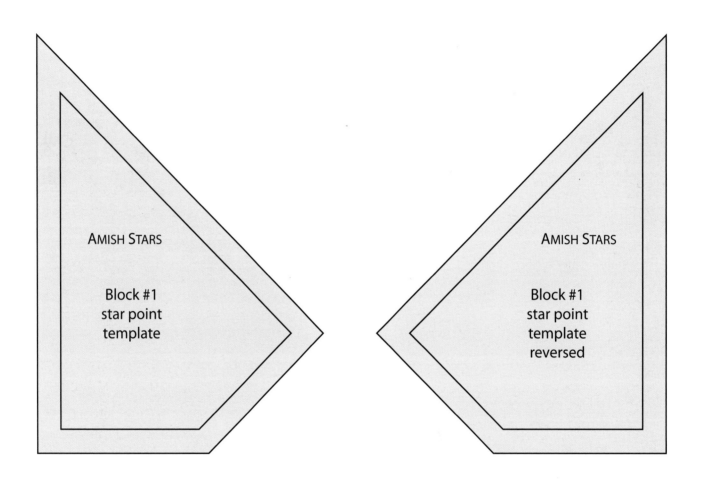

AMISH STARS

Block #1
star point
template

AMISH STARS

Block #1
star point
template
reversed

AMISH STARS, 72" X 72" • made by Daphne Greig

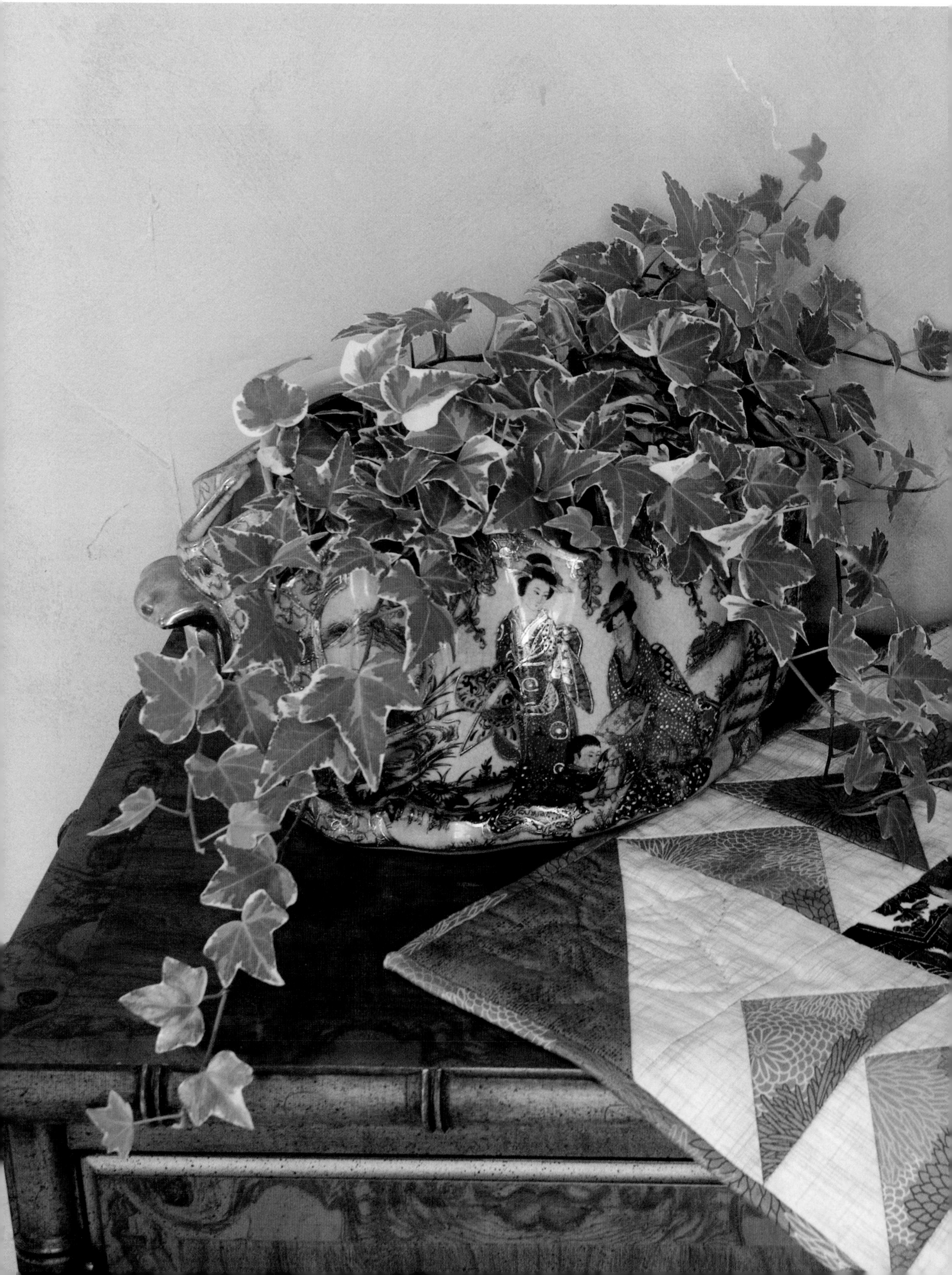

Asian Flight

Finished size: 20" x 20"

What can you make with only four fat quarters? Plenty of projects! This table topper is one. For more, see the Take Four Table Runner on page 47 and the Fishy Fishy wallhanging on page 78.

Feature a large scale print for the center panel and then select three coordinating fabrics to surround it.

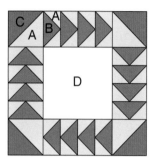

Fabric Requirements

Fabric A (light)	1 fat quarter
Fabric B (medium)	1 fat quarter
Fabric C (medium/dark)	1 fat quarter
Fabric D (large scale print)	1 fat quarter
Backing	24" x 24"
Batting	24" x 24"

Cutting Instructions

Fabric A (light)—*cut from the **long** side*
1 strip 5⅞" wide, cut into 2 squares
3 strips 3⅜" wide, cut into 16 squares

Fabric B (medium)—*cut from the **short** side*
2 strips 6¼" wide, cut into 4 squares
5 strips 1½" wide (for binding)

Fabric C (medium/dark)—*cut from the **long** side*
1 strip 5⅞" wide, cut into 2 squares

Fabric D (large scale print)
1 square 10½" x 10½"

Making the quilt

To make the flying geese units, first mark a diagonal line on the wrong side of the 3⅜" A squares.

Layer two marked A squares right sides together with one B square as shown. Sew ¼" on each side of the marked line. Cut along the marked line and press the small triangles away from the large triangles to complete 2 units.

Place another A square right sides together on both of the units as shown, and sew ¼" on each side of the marked line. Cut along the line and press the small triangles away from the large triangle. You now have 4 flying geese units.

Make 16
Flying Geese units

Repeat with the remaining A and B squares to make a total of 16 flying geese units.

Make 4 rows of 4 flying geese units as shown. Press seams open.

Make 4 rows

Sew a row of flying geese units to opposite sides of the D square as shown. Press seams toward the D square.

Draw a diagonal line on the wrong side of the 5⅞" A squares. Place right sides together with the C squares.

Sew ¼" on either side of the drawn line and cut apart. Make 4 half-square triangles.

Make 4
half-square triangles

Sew a half-square triangle to both ends of the remaining flying geese rows. Press the seam allowances toward the half-square triangles.

Make 2

Sew to the top and bottom as shown.

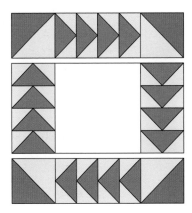

Layer the top with the backing and batting and quilt the layers by hand or machine .

Join the B strips with diagonal seams and use your favorite method to bind the raw edges of your quilt.

Take Four Table Runner

Finished size: 14½" x 42"

This great little runner only needs only four fabrics, including the binding. What could be easier?

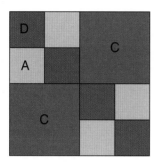

Fabric Requirements

Fabric A (light)	1 fat quarter
Fabric B (light/medium)	1 fat quarter
Fabric C (medium)	1 fat quarter
Fabric D (dark)	1 fat quarter
Backing	18" x 46"
Batting	18" x 46"

Cutting Instructions

Fabric A (light)—*cut from the long side*
2 strips 3" wide, cut into 12 squares

Fabric B (light/medium)
1 square 15½" x 15½" cut in quarters diagonally (for setting triangles)

Fabric C (medium)—*cut from the long side*
2 strips 5½" wide, cut into 6 squares

Fabric D (dark)—*cut from the long side*
2 strips 3" wide, cut into 12 squares
6 strips 1½" wide (for the binding)

Making the table runner

Join pairs of A and D squares. Press the seams open.

Join 2 A/D pairs to make 6 four-patch units as shown. Press the seams open.

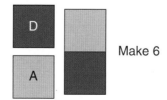

Make 6

Join each four-patch unit with a C square. Press the seams open.

Join the units to make 3 blocks as shown. Press the seams open.

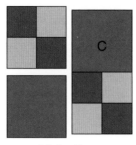

Make 3

Lay out the blocks and the 4 setting triangles as shown. Join the blocks and triangles in rows, then join the rows. Press the seams open.

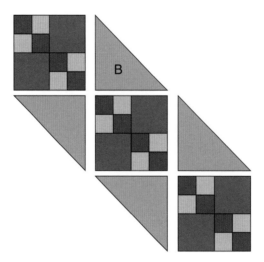

Layer the runner top with the backing and batting and quilt the layers by hand or machine.

Susan chose to stitch in the ditch around the blocks and use a floral pattern in the setting triangles.

Join the D strips with diagonal seams and use your favorite method to bind the raw edges of your runner.

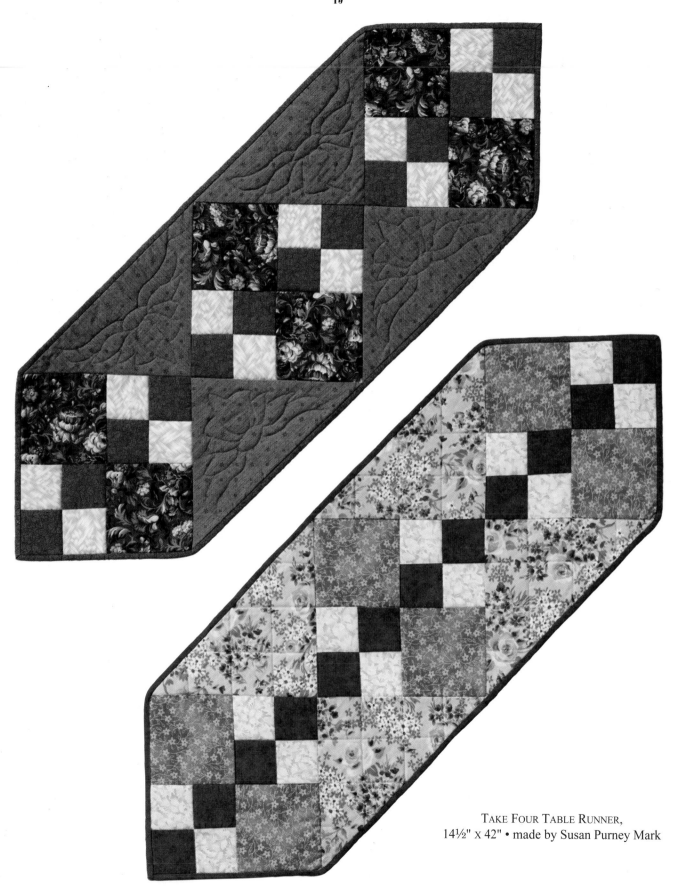

TAKE FOUR TABLE RUNNER,
14½" x 42" • made by Susan Purney Mark

Desert Nights

Finished quilt: 62½" x 62½" ~ Finished block: 6½" x 6½"

Turn two colors and some foundation-pieced blocks into this intricate-looking graphic design. You will have perfect points with this method. Select a range of values of two colors for this quilt. Daphne used blue and orange, complementary colors on the color wheel. Her orange choices include gold, rust, and brown and she selected light/medium through very dark values of each color.

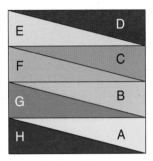

Spikes block

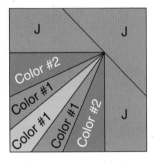

Border corner block

Fabric Requirements

Color #1 (orange)

Fabric A (light/medium)	3 fat quarters
Fabric B (medium)	3 fat quarters
Fabric C (medium/dark)	3 fat quarters
Fabric D (very dark)	3 fat quarters

Color #2 (blue)

Fabric E (light/medium)	3 fat quarters
Fabric F (medium)	3 fat quarters
Fabric G (medium/dark)	3 fat quarters
Fabric H (very dark)	3 fat quarters
Fabric I (third inner border–light)	1 fat quarter
Fabric J (outer border & binding)	1⅓ yards
Backing	4 yards
Batting	70" x 70"

Spikes Block Cutting Instructions

For cutting, the fat quarters are arranged in stacks to match the piecing sequence of the spikes blocks.

Make 3 stacks of D, E, C, and F fat quarters, in that order, with D on top, all right side up.

*From the **short** side of the 3 fat quarter stacks* cut 16 strips 3¼" wide (6 from the first two stacks, 4 from the third stack). Set aside the remainder of the third stack for later.

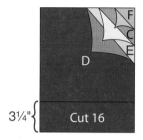

Cut 2 rectangles 3¼" x 8½" from each stack of strips, then cut each stack of rectangles diagonally, starting and ending ½" from the edges as shown for a total of 256 wedge triangles.

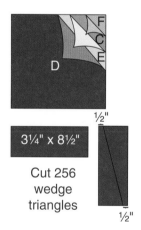

*Each stack of triangles is in the right order for sewing the **first** 4 segments of each spikes block.*

Make 3 stacks of B, G, A, and H fat quarters, in that order, with B on top, all right side up.

*From the **short** side of the 3 fat quarter stacks,* cut 16 strips 3¼" wide (6 from the first two stacks, 4 from the third stack). Set aside the remainder of the third stack for later.

Cut 2 rectangles 3¼" x 8½" from each stack of strips, then cut each stack of rectangles diagonally, starting and ending ½" from the edges as shown, for a total of 256 wedge triangles.

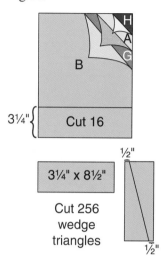

*Each stack of triangles is in the right order for sewing the **last** 4 segments of each spikes block.*

Corner Block Cutting Instructions

Select one of the color #1 remainders and cut a 2½" wide strip from which you cut 2 rectangles 2½" x 8½". Cut the rectangles in half diagonally (for the center spike in the corner blocks).

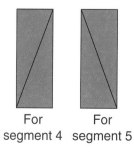

Select one of the color #2 remainders and cut 2 strips 3½" wide from which you cut 4 rectangles 3½" x 7" (for segments 4 and 5 of the corner blocks; see the template on page 57). Cut the rectangles in half diagonally as shown.

For
segment 4   segment 5

Select another of the color #1 remainders and cut 2 strips 2½" wide from which you cut 4 rectangles 2½" x 8". Cut the rectangles in half diagonally (for segments 2 and 3 in the corner blocks).

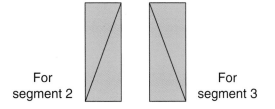

From the J yardage, cut a strip 2¾" wide selvage to selvage. The strip will be used for segments 6 and 7 of the corner blocks.

Cut 2 squares 6". Cut the squares in half diagonally (for segment 8).

Border Cutting Instructions

From the longest side of the 2 color #1 remainders cut:
5 strips 1½" wide from each (total of 10 strips for the first inner border).

From the longest side of the last 3 color #2 remainders cut:
4 strips 1½" wide (total 12 strips) for the second inner border.

*From the **long** side of the I fat quarter* cut:
9 strips 1¾" wide (for the third inner border).

Cut fabric J yardage, selvage to selvage into:
7 strips 2½" wide (for the outer border)
7 strips 2¼" wide (for the binding).

Making the blocks

Trace or copy 64 spikes block foundation templates found on page 56.

Select a D/E/C/F stack of triangles for segments 1–4. Sew to the foundation. Select a B/G/A/H stack of triangles for segments 5–8. Sew to the foundation. Make 64 blocks.

Trim the blocks to 7" square and remove the foundation papers.

Trace or copy 4 corner block foundation templates (page 57).

Piece the corner blocks with the triangles and border pieces cut for them. Make 4 corner blocks.

Trim the blocks to 7" square and remove the foundation papers.

Assembling the quilt

Arrange 36 spikes blocks in 6 rows as shown. Sew the blocks together in rows and then sew the rows together, pressing seams alternately.

Join the 1½" color #1 strips end-to-end alternating colors to make one continuous strip.

Add the inner borders log-cabin style, so the different fabrics in the long strip will match as they go around the corners of the quilt. Press all seam allowances toward the border.

Measure the length of the quilt through the center and cut a border piece that measurement from the long strip. Sew it to the left side of the quilt.

Measure the width of the quilt through the center, cut, and sew the strip to the bottom of the quilt.

Measure the length of the quilt through the center, cut, and sew the strip to the right side of the quilt.

Measure the width of the quilt through the center, cut, and sew the strip to the top of the quilt.

Join the 1½" color #2 strips end-to-end alternating colors to make one continuous strip.

Measuring through the center, cut and sew the second inner border strips to the quilt log-cabin style as before, pressing the seam allowance toward the border.

Join the 1¾" third inner border strips end-to-end with diagonal seams to make one continuous strip.

Measuring through the center, cut and sew the third inner border strips to the quilt log-cabin style as before, pressing the seam allowances toward the border.

Arrange and sew the remaining spikes blocks into 4 border rows of 7 blocks each. Sew borders to the sides.

Add border corner blocks to the remaining border rows, positioning them as shown, and add them to the top and bottom of the quilt.

Join the 2½" outer border strips end-to-end with diagonal seams to make one continuous strip. Measure, cut, and sew the outer border to the quilt as before.

Layer the quilt top with backing and batting and quilt the layers by hand or machine.

Daphne quilted random wavy lines over all the blocks and wavy lines inside each border.

Use the 2¼" binding strips and your favorite method to bind the raw edges of your quilt.

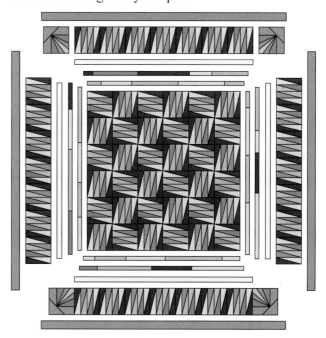

DESERT NIGHTS
62½" x 62½" • made by Daphne Greig

DESERT NIGHTS

Spikes block foundation – 7″ square unfinished

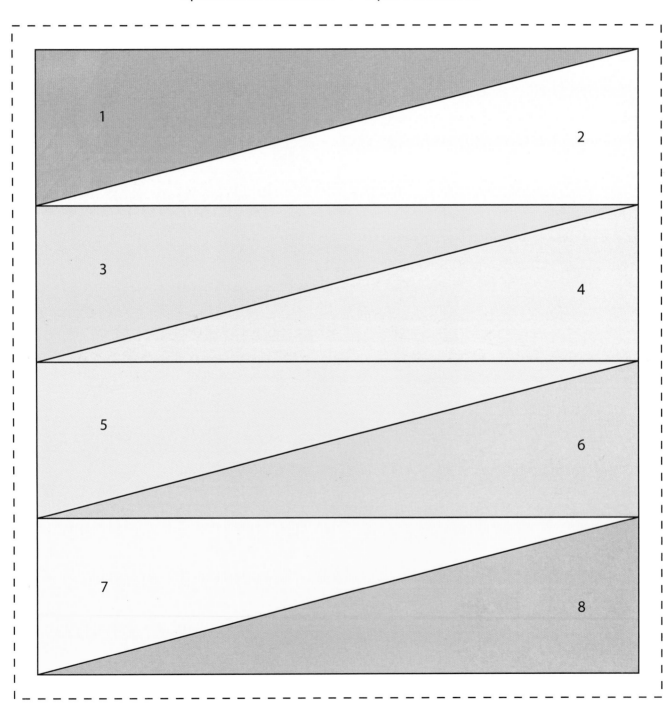

DESERT NIGHTS

Corner block foundation – 7" square unfinished

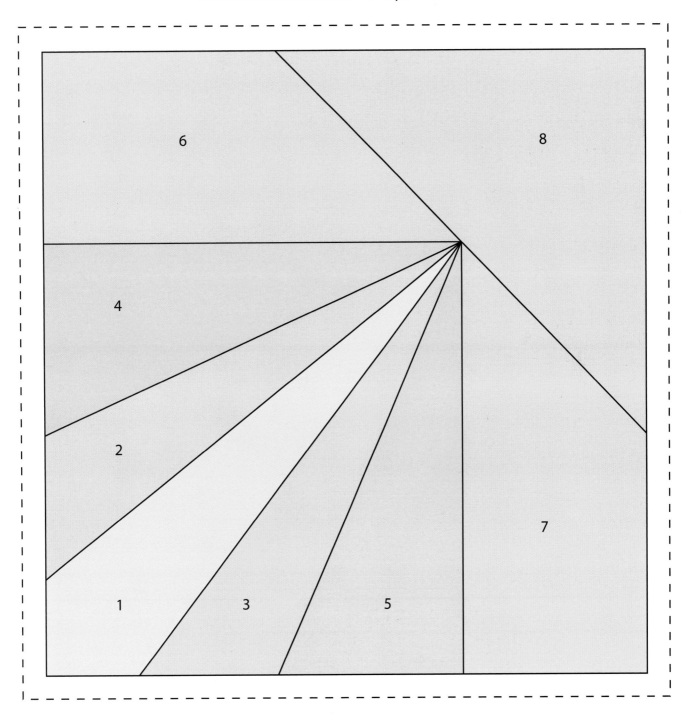

Strip Doodles

Finished quilt: 40¼" x 51½" ⌒ Finished block: 9¾"

Make this simple and speedy quilt to welcome a new addition to your family or to your neighborhood. Large scale prints are fun to use because each block will be different and at the same time, coordinated. It will look great in bright prints or soft pastels—or make one of each.

Fabric Requirements

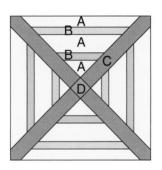

Fabric A (large scale coordinating prints)	6 fat quarters
Fabric B (tone-on-tone prints, different colors)	2 fat quarters
Fabric C (accent, different colors)	2 fat quarters
Fabric D (cornerstones)	1 fat quarter
Fabric E (sashing, different colors)	2 fat quarters
Fabric F (border, different colors)	2 fat quarters
Binding	½ yard
Backing	2⅞ yards
Batting	46" x 57"

Cutting Instructions

Fabric A (large scale prints)—*cut from the **long** side*
*from **two** fat quarters cut* – 8 strips 2" wide (total of 16)
*from **two** fat quarters cut* – 8 strips 1¾" wide (total of 16)
*from **two** fat quarters cut* – 8 strips 1¼" wide (total of 16)

Fabric B (tone-on-tone prints)—*cut from the **long** side*
16 strips 1" wide (total of 32)

Fabric C (accents)—*cut from the **short** side*
12 strips 1½" wide, cut into 24 rectangles 1½" x 8½" (total of 48)

Fabric D (cornerstones)—*cut from the **long** side*
1 strip 1½" wide, cut into 12 squares
2 strips 2" wide, cut into 20 squares
1 strip 3" wide, cut into 4 squares

Fabric E (sashing)—*cut from **long** side*
8 strips 2" wide (total of 16) wide, cut into 15 rectangles 2" x 10¼" for horizontal sashing
16 rectangles 2" x 10¼" for vertical sashing

■ ■ **Fabric F** (border)—*cut from **long** side*
*from **one** fat quarter cut* – 4 strips 3" wide (top and bottom borders)
*from **one** fat quarter cut* – 5 strips 3" wide (side borders)

Binding—*cut from selvage to selvage*
cut 5 strips 2¼" wide

Making the blocks

Make 8 matching pairs of strip-sets by sewing 3 widths of fabric A strips (1¼", 1½", and 2" wide) and fabric B 1" wide strips together as shown, for a total of 16 strip-sets.

Use 3 different widths of fabric A strips in each strip-set with different color tone-on-tone strips between them. Use a different arrangement of the widths in the different pairs of strip-sets.

Press seams to one side after each strip is sewn. This will help keep the strip-set straight. The strip-sets will measure 5" wide.

A	2"
B - color 2	
A	1¾"
B - color 1	
A	1¼"

Make 16 strip-sets in matching pairs

Copy the triangle template on page 62 and cut it out. For easy cutting, tape the triangle template onto the ruler corner and cut out 3 triangles from each strip-set as shown. Handle bias edges of triangles carefully so they don't become stretched.

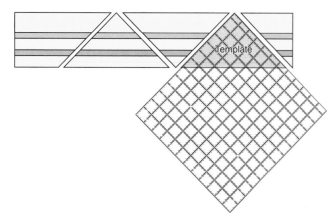

Important: Be sure to cut 4 pairs of strips with the same color fabric B near the wide bottom of the triangle and 4 pairs with the other color near the bottom of the triangle. Following these instructions will give you 24 matching triangle pairs.

Using 2 pairs of matching (fabric B) triangles for each block, sew a fabric C 1½" x 8½" rectangle between the triangles as shown. Press seam allowances toward fabric C.

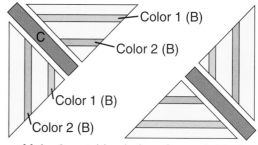

Make 2 matching halves for each block

Sew fabric D 1½" squares between the matching fabric C 1½" x 8½" rectangles as shown. Press seam allowances toward fabric C.

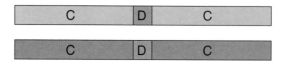

Sew this unit between the corner units as shown. Press. Trim the block to measure 10¼" square. Make 6 blocks with each fabric C color, a total of 12 blocks.

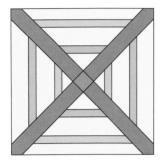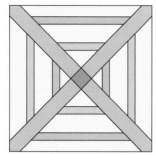

Arrange blocks into rows, alternating fabric C colors as shown. Sew matching E vertical sashing rectangles between the blocks and on the ends as shown. Press seam allowance toward sashing.

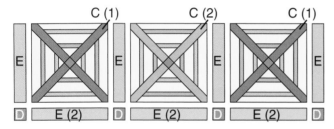

Sew matching E horizontal sashing rectangles and fabric D 2" squares together as shown. Press seam allowance toward sashing. Then sew these units between the rows and on top and bottom of the quilt top. Press seam allowances toward the sashing units.

Adding the borders

Sew the matching 3" wide border strips end-to-end with diagonal seams. Press seam allowances open.

Measure the length of the quilt through the center and cut 2 matching border strips to that measurement.

Before adding the side borders, measure the width of the quilt through the center and cut the remaining 2 border strips to that measurement.

Sew the fabric D 3" squares onto each end of these border strips. Press seam allowances toward the border fabric.

Sew the side borders to the quilt, then sew the top and bottom borders to the quilt. Press seam allowances toward the outer edge.

Layer the quilt top with backing and batting, then quilt the layers by hand or machine.

Daphne quilted a wave pattern in the middle of the C strips and the sashing rectangles. She quilted the same pattern three times in the borders.

Join the 2¼" wide binding strips with diagonal seams and use your favorite method to bind the raw edges of your quilt.

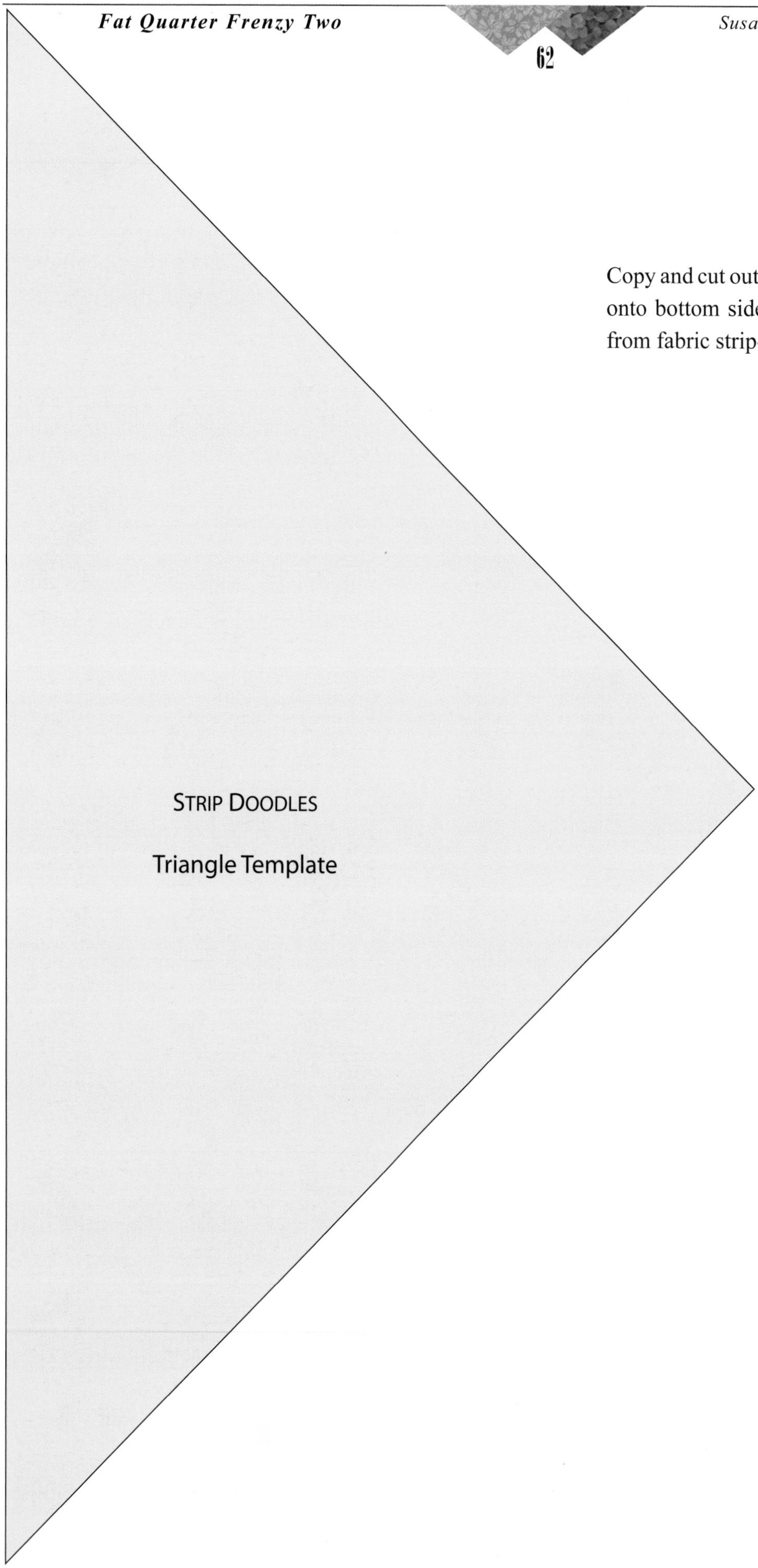

Copy and cut out triangle template. Tape triangle onto bottom side of ruler and cut out triangles from fabric strip-set.

STRIP DOODLES

Triangle Template

STRIP DOODLES, 40¼" x 51½" • made by Daphne Greig

Shattered Garden

Finished quilt: 57" x 57" ⌐ Finished block: 12" x 12"

These blocks create the appearance of a flower garden and trellis, making a lovely lap-sized quilt or wallhanging. Use a wide variety of floral prints, so the flowers in your quilt will always be blooming.

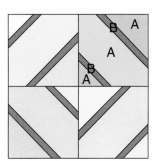

Fabric Requirements

Fabric A (mixed floral prints)	11 fat quarters
Fabric B (mixed greens)	5 fat quarters
Binding & inner border	¾ yard
Backing	3⅝ yards
Batting	63" x 63"

Cutting Instructions

Fabric A—*cut from the **long** side*
2 strips 6½" wide (total of 22 strips)
1 strip 4" wide (total of 11 strips)

Fabric B—*cut from the **long** side*
12 strips 1" wide (total of 60 strips)

Inner border and binding
6 strips 1½" wide
6 strips 2¼" wide

Making the blocks

Layer the A strips into groups of 4–6, aligning their raw edges. Make sure that the same fabrics are not layered on top of one another.

You will cut and sew one group of strips at a time.

Cut through the layers at a 45-degree angle to make segments in varying widths from 2" to 4" wide. The measurements do not need to be exact but the angle should be precise. Use the 45-degree line on your ruler.

Rearrange the cut segments as follows:

Stack 1: Leave this stack of segments alone.
Stack 2: Take one off the top and move it to the bottom.
Stack 3: Take two off the top and move them to the bottom.
Stack 4: Take three off the top and move them to the bottom.

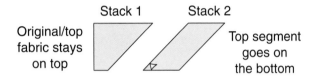

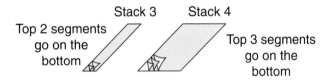

Continue in this manner until all but the first of the stacks have been rearranged.

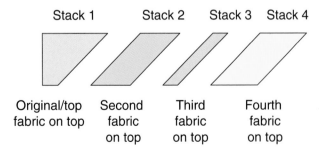

Sew a B strip to the diagonal edge of the top segment in stack 1, making sure the strip extends at least 1" beyond both edges. Press the seam allowance toward the B strip, then trim the strip even with the top and bottom edges of the segment.

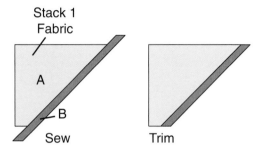

Join the top segment from the second stack to the trimmed B strip, making certain the edges of the segments will line up when sewn. There should be a ¼" triangle of fabric extending beyond both edges of the trimmed unit when you sew on the next segment.

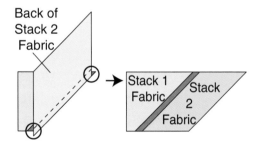

Continue sewing A segments and B strips until you have used the top segment from each stack to make a complete strip-unit. Always press the seam allowances toward the B strips.

Sew all the segments in one layer before proceeding to the next layer.

Repeat these steps for all the groups of A strips, cutting into segments, rearranging the stacks, and sewing the A segments and B strips to make strip-units. Make 22.

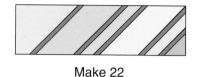

Make 22

Cut 6½" squares from the strip-units. You need a total of 64 squares.

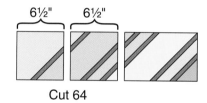

Cut 64

Select 4 squares for each block so that the B strips *do not* line up. Lay out all the blocks as shown before joining the squares, making sure there is an even distribution of colors and values.

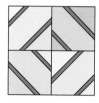

Make 16

When you are satisfied with the distribution, join the squares into blocks.

Lay out the completed blocks in 4 rows of 4 blocks each, rotating and rearranging them until you are happy with the way they look. Sew the blocks into rows and join the rows. Press the seam allowances open.

Making the borders

Join 6 inner border strips end-to-end with diagonal seams. Press seam allowances open.

Measure the length and width of the quilt through the center. These two measurements should be the same.

Cut 2 inner border pieces this measurement from the long strip. Sew them to the sides of the quilt. Press the seam allowances toward the border.

For the outer border cut 32 rectangles 4" x 6½" and 4 squares from the 4" A strips.

Sew 8 of the rectangles together, end-to-end along the 4" sides to form a long strip. The strip length should equal the length and width measurements of the quilt. Make 4 strips like this.

Make 4

Check that the length of the pieced outer border strips is the same as the length/width measurement of the quilt. Adjust as needed by trimming or adding an extra rectangle and then trimming to size.

Sew 2 outer border strips to the sides of the quilt.

Measure the width of the quilt, including both borders and cut 2 strips that length from the long inner border strip. Sew them to the top and bottom of the quilt. Press the seam allowances toward the border.

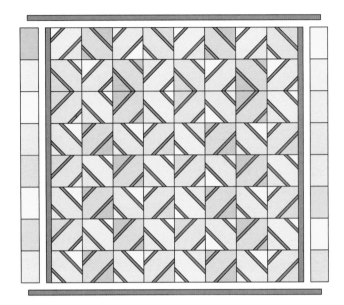

Add a 1½" wide B inner border strip and a 4" A square to both ends of 2 of the remaining outer border strips as shown. Press the seam allowances open.

Make 2

Sew these strips to the top and bottom of the quilt.

Layer the quilt top with the backing and batting, then quilt the layers by hand or machine.

Susan quilted in the ditch around the blocks and then quilted a curving pattern inside each block.

Use the 2¼" binding strips and your favorite method to bind the raw edges of your quilt.

SHATTERED GARDEN, 57" x 57" • made by Susan Purney Mark

Heather's Choice

Finished quilt: 50" x 66" ⌒ Finished block: 8" x 8"

Purples and greens lend themselves to a soft color combination that has a touch of the Scottish Highlands. Rotate the blocks to try many possible arrangements.

Fabric Requirements

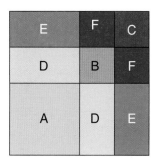

Fabric A (light green)	3 fat quarters
Fabric B (medium green)	1 fat quarter
Fabric C (dark green)	1 fat quarter
Fabric D (light purple)	3 fat quarters
Fabric E (medium purple)	3 fat quarters
Fabric F (dark purple)	2 fat quarters
Inner border	⅜ yard
Outer border	1½ yards
Binding	½ yard
Backing	3½ yards
Batting	56" x 72"

Cutting Instructions

Fabric A—*cut from the **long** side*
3 strips 4½" wide cut into 35 squares

Fabric B, C, & F—*cut from the **long** side*
5 strips 2½" wide

Fabric D & E—*cut from the **long** side*
6 strips 2½" wide

Making the blocks

Sew B and F strips together to make 5 strip-sets. Press seam allowances toward the dark strips. From the strip-sets, cut 35 segments 2½" wide.

2½"

Cut 35   Make 5 strip-sets

Sew C and F strips together to make 5 strip-sets. Press seam allowances toward the dark strips. From the strip-sets, cut 35 segments 2½" wide.

Cut 35   Make 5 strip-sets

Join the segments to make 35 four-patch units as shown. Press the seam allowance open.

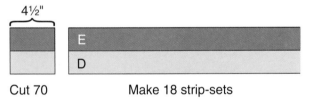

Make 35

Sew D and E strips together to make 18 strip-sets. Press seam allowances toward the *light* strips. From the strip-sets, cut 70 segments 4½" wide.

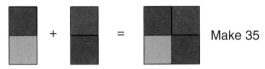

Cut 70   Make 18 strip-sets

Join a four-patch unit, the D/E segments, and A squares to form the blocks as shown, paying close attention to the position of the dark squares in the four-patch units. Press the seam allowances open. Make 35 blocks.

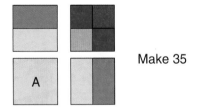

Make 35

Arrange the blocks in 7 rows of 5 blocks each as shown or try rotating them to create a different arrangement. Sew the blocks into rows and join the rows. Press all seam allowances open for a flatter quilt.

Adding the borders

From the inner border fabric, cut 6 strips 1½" wide, selvage to selvage.

Sew these strips together end-to-end with diagonal seams to make one long strip.

Measure the length of the quilt through the center and cut 2 inner border pieces that length from the long strip. Sew them to the sides of the quilt. Press the seam allowances toward the border.

Measure the width of the quilt through the center and cut 2 pieces that length from the long strip. Sew these to the top and bottom. Press the seam allowances toward the border.

From the outer border fabric, cut 7 strips 4½" wide, selvage to selvage. Sew the strips together end-to-end with diagonal seams to make one long strip. Trim seam allowances to ¼" and press open.

Measure, cut, and add the outer border to the quilt in the same way as the inner border.

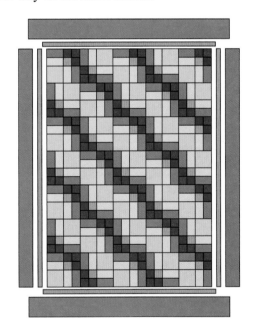

Layer the quilt top with the backing and batting, then quilt the layers by hand or machine.

Susan quilted a diagonal leaf line over the center of the quilt. A similar design was repeated in the border.

From the binding fabric, cut 7 strips 2¼" wide, selvage to selvage. Use these strips and your favorite method to bind the raw edges of your quilt.

HEATHER'S CHOICE, 50" x 66" • made by Susan Purney Mark

Cuddles & Playtime

Finished quilt: 45" x 55" ↝ Finished block: 10" x 10"

Made in bright pastels, this quilt is perfect for a baby's room or for a child moving to a larger bed. The simple block makes sewing easy and quick, and a favorite grandma is sure to have a great collection of fat quarters.

Fabric Requirements

Fabric A (blue)	3 fat quarters
Fabric B (purple)	3 fat quarters
Fabric C (yellow)	3 fat quarters
Fabric D (pink)	3 fat quarters
Fabric E (green)	2 fat quarters
Fabric F (turquoise)	2 fat quarters
Fabric G (white)	3 fat quarters
Binding	½ yard
Backing	3 yards
Batting	53" x 63" low-loft cotton

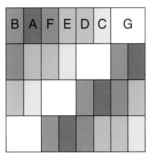

Cutting Instructions

Fabric A, B, C, D (blue, purple, yellow, pink)—*cut from the **long** side*
*from **two** fat quarters of each color cut* – 7 strips 1¾" wide (total of 56)
*from **one** fat quarter of each color cut* – 3 strips 3" wide (for borders; total of 12)

Fabric E & F (green & turquoise)—*cut from the **long** side*
*from **two** fat quarters of each color cut* – 7 strips 1¾" wide (total of 56)
2 squares 3" x 3" (for borders; total of 4)

Fabric G (white)—*cut from the **long** side*
14 strips 3" wide, cut into 80 squares

Binding
cut 6 strips, selvage to selvage, 2¼" wide

Making the blocks

Make strip-sets with the 1¾" strips as follows:

A & B – make 14

C & D – make 14

E & F – make 14

Press the seams open.

Cut each strip-set into 6 segments 3" wide. You need 80 segments of each color combination for a total of 240 segments.

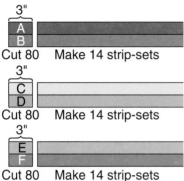

Join 12 segments and 4 G 3" squares as shown to make 20 blocks. Press all seam allowances open.

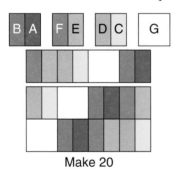

Make 20

Arrange the completed blocks, following the quilt assembly diagram to the right. Sew the blocks together in rows then join the rows. Press all seam allowances open.

Adding the borders

For the 4 borders, join 3 matching 3" wide border strips with diagonal seams.

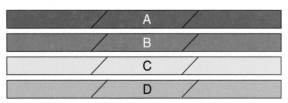

Measure the length of the quilt through the middle and cut 2 border strips to that measurement.

Before adding the side borders, measure the width of the quilt through the center and cut the remaining 2 border strips to that measurement.

Sew the E and F squares to the ends of these 2 borders.

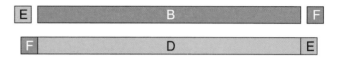

Sew the side borders to the quilt, then sew the top and bottom borders to the quilt.

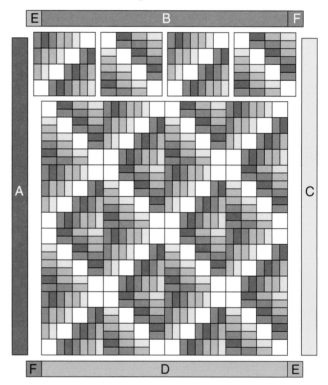

Sandwich the quilt top with backing and batting and quilt the layers by hand or machine.

Suggested designs include floral and vine motifs or an overall diagonal pattern.

Join the binding strips with diagonal seams and use your favorite method to bind the raw edges of your quilt.

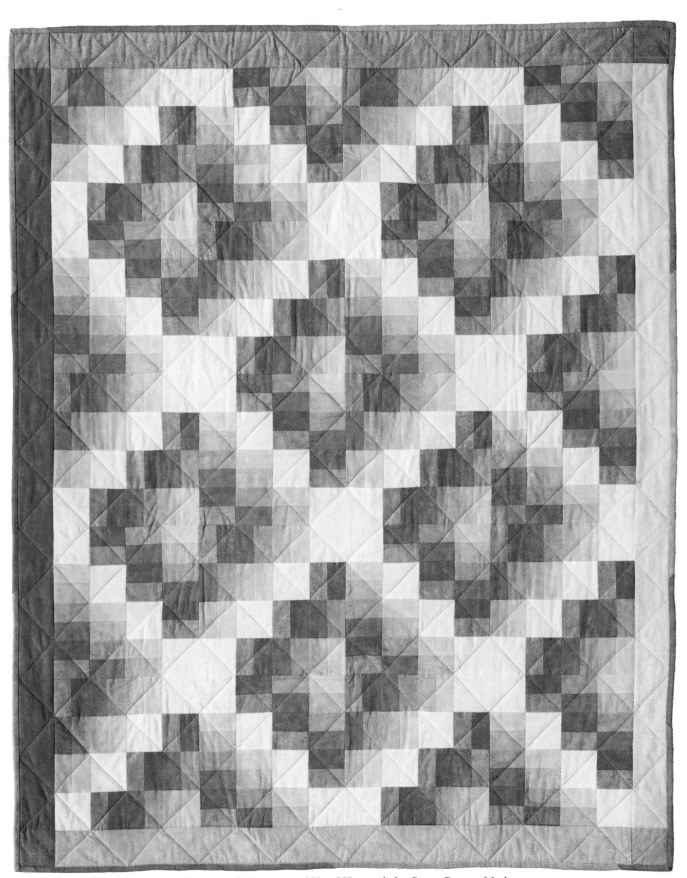

CUDDLES & PLAYTIME, 45" x 55" • made by Susan Purney Mark

ONLY TAKES
4
FAT QUARTERS

Fishy Fishy

Finished quilt: 10½" x 25" ↝ Made by Daphne Greig

This project is great for batiks, seaside prints, or something wild and crazy. The simple pieced background and easy mitered borders mean that you can have it finished quickly. This can be done by hand appliqué or by fusing. Supplies are given for both methods.

Appliqué Supplies

Scissors

We recommend a sharp pair of fabric scissors for cutting appliqué shapes.

Thread

We like a lighter cotton (60 weight), rayon, or polyester thread for machine appliqué. For hand appliqué, we like to use silk thread. You will need appliqué needles for hand appliqué.

Pins

Small appliqué pins are useful for hand appliqué. Select the ones with small heads. They are easy to see and still small enough that your thread won't catch on them while you are stitching.

Template Plastic

We prefer the gridded template plastic marked in ⅛" increments. It is transparent so you can trace patterns accurately. We use paper scissors for cutting our traced shapes.

Template plastic is also useful for placing appliqués on your background fabric. Tape the background fabric to your work surface. Trace the appliqué design on the plastic, then align the tracing on the background fabric. Tape the plastic to the work surface on one side only. Lift the plastic to slip the appliqué pieces underneath.

Fusible Web

We use paper-backed fusible web for machine appliqué projects. We like one with paper backing on both sides. Use a Teflon® pressing sheet for appliqué when working with fusibles to protect both the ironing board and your iron, and follow the manufacturer's directions for iron temperature and fusing time.

There are several weights available. Choose the one that is best for your project. For example, lightweight fusibles work well for lap quilts and larger, when you would like the fabric to remain soft. Heavier weights are fine for wall quilts since the fabric will feel a bit stiff after fusing. Be sure to choose an easily sewn fusible web if you plan to sew the edges of your appliqué shapes.

Fabric Requirements

Fabric A (light)	1 fat quarter for background and binding
Fabric B (medium)	1 fat quarter for background and binding
Fabric C (purple)	1 fat quarter for fish, border, and binding
Fabric D (green)	1 fat quarter for seaweed, border, and binding
Backing	⅞ yard
Batting	24" x 29"
Fusible web	1 yard

Cutting Instructions

Fabric A and B—*cut from the long side*

4 strips 3½" wide (total of 8)

2 strips 1½" wide (total of 4) for binding

Fabric C and D—*cut from the long side*

2 strips 3½" wide (total of 4) for border

2 strips 1½" wide (total of 4) for binding

Background Assembly

Make 4 strip-sets with fabric A and fabric B 3½" strips. Press the seam allowance open.

Cut 24 segments 3½" wide.

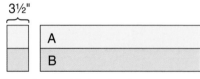

3½"

A

B

Cut 24   Make 4 strip-sets

Lay out the segments in a checkerboard arrangement. Sew 6 segments into 4 rows, then sew the rows together. Press seam allowances open.

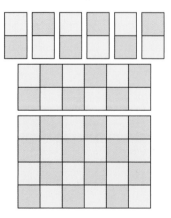

Adding the borders

For the borders, join the fabric C 3½" strips with a diagonal seam. Join the fabric D 3½" strips with a diagonal seam. Press seam allowances open.

Layer the fabric C and D border strips right sides together and trim the left end of both strips with a 45-degree angle cut.

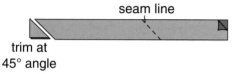

Mark a dot on the wrong side of each strip ¼" away from both edges as shown. Mark another dot on the wrong side ¼" away from both edges on the lower left corner of the background. These dots mark where the seams for the border strips meet at the corner of the background.

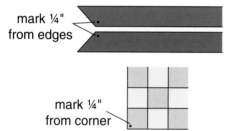

Lay the fabric C border strip along the bottom of the quilt, right sides together, aligning the raw edges and the dots. Starting at the dot, sew the fabric C border to the background.

Do not sew into the seam allowances beyond the dots.

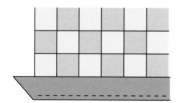

Press the border away from the quilt. Add the fabric D border strip to the left side of the quilt in the same manner.

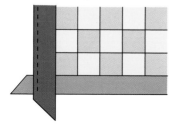

Fold the quilt on the diagonal so that the borders line up, one on top of the other. Join the 2 border strips along the diagonal cut edge. Press the seam allowances open to complete the quilt top.

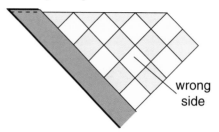

Appliqué

Use a pencil to trace each of the appliqué shapes onto the paper side of fusible web (see pages 82–91). Cut out ⅛" beyond the traced line.

Following the manufacturer's direction, fuse the web pieces to the wrong side of the C and D fabrics.

Cut the fabric shapes exactly on the drawn line with small, sharp-pointed scissors. Place the appliqué pieces on the background, weaving the seaweed in front of and behind the fish. Fuse in place.

Layer the quilt with backing and batting. Pin or baste well. Appliqué the pieces and quilt the layers at the same time, using invisible thread or a colored embroidery-weight thread and a small zigzag stitch. Stitch all the way around each piece and around the cutouts in the fish.

Finishing

Quilt the background and borders by using the seaweed shapes or wavy lines as a theme.

Sew the 1½" binding strips to the quilt, matching the binding seams to the quilt seams where the colors change.

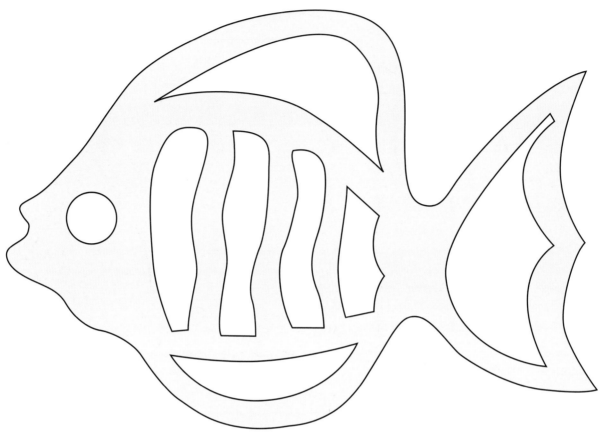

FISHY FISHY

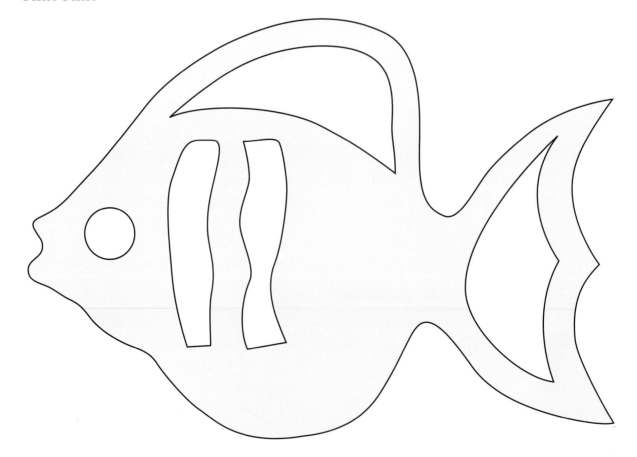

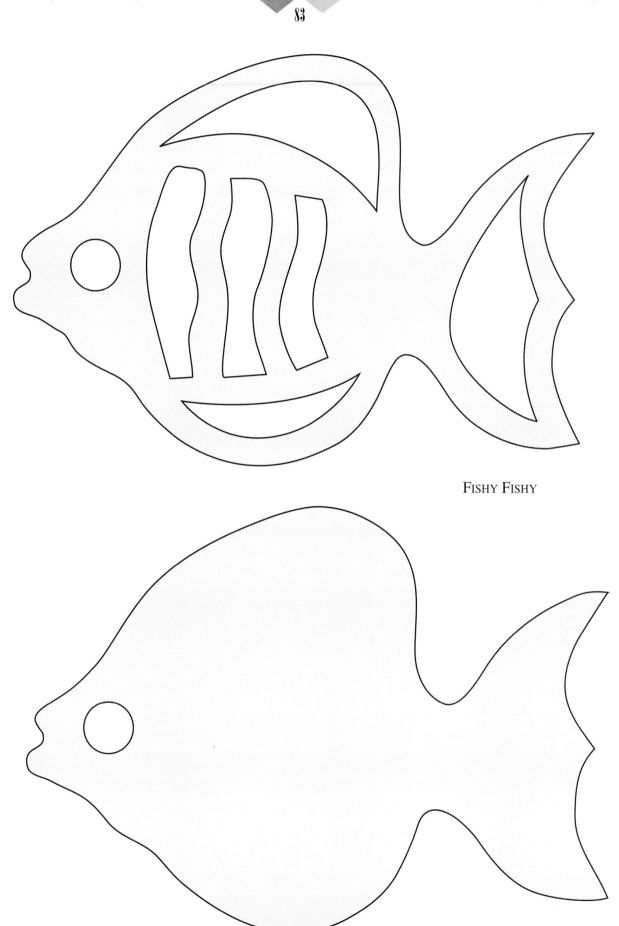

FISHY FISHY

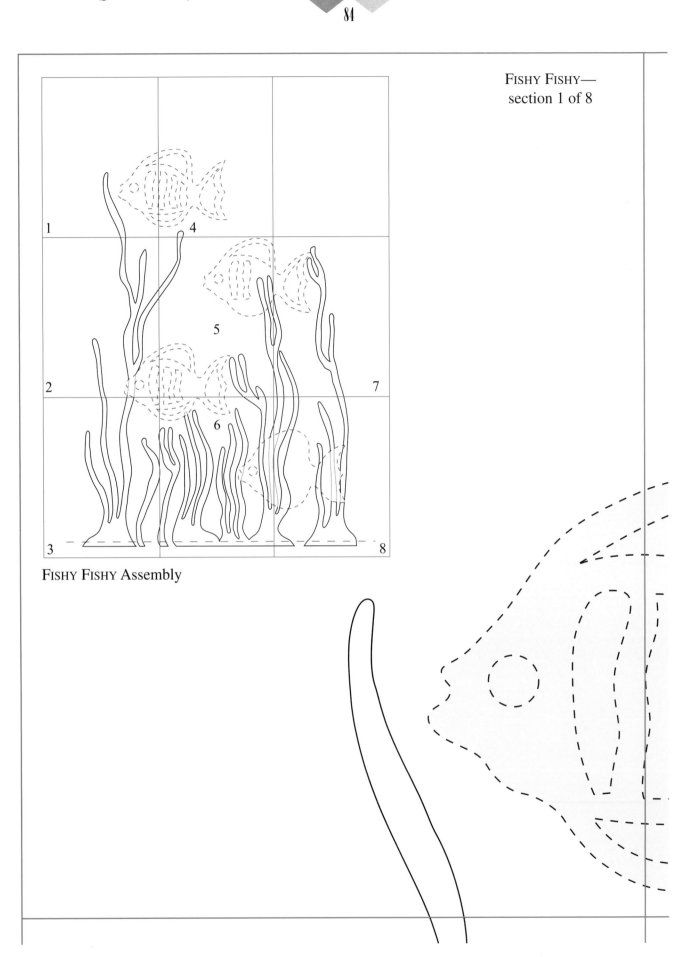

FISHY FISHY—
section 1 of 8

FISHY FISHY Assembly

FISHY FISHY—
    section 2 of 8

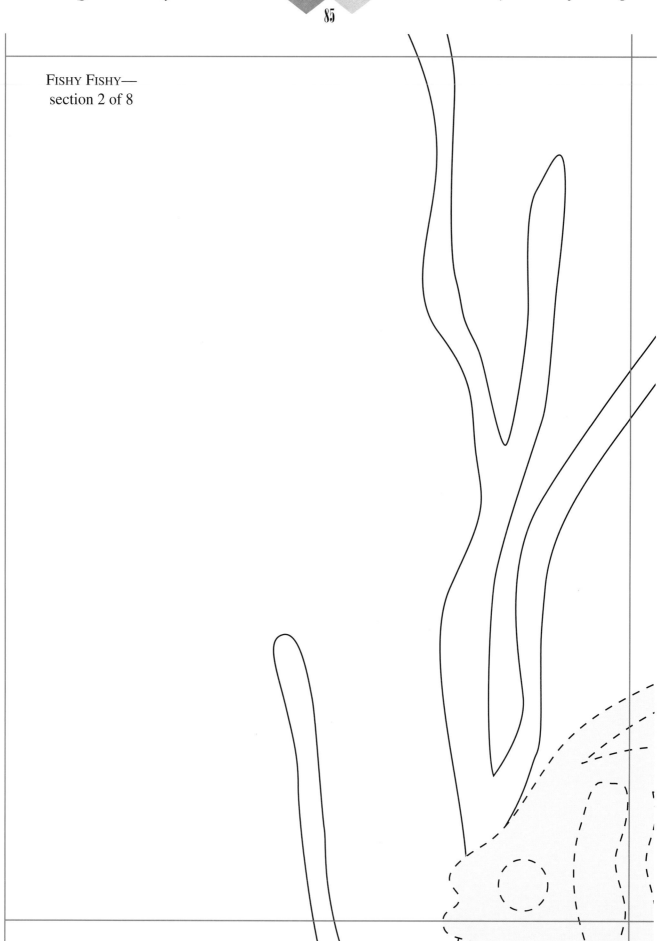

FISHY FISHY—
section 3 of 8

FISHY FISHY—
section 4 of 8

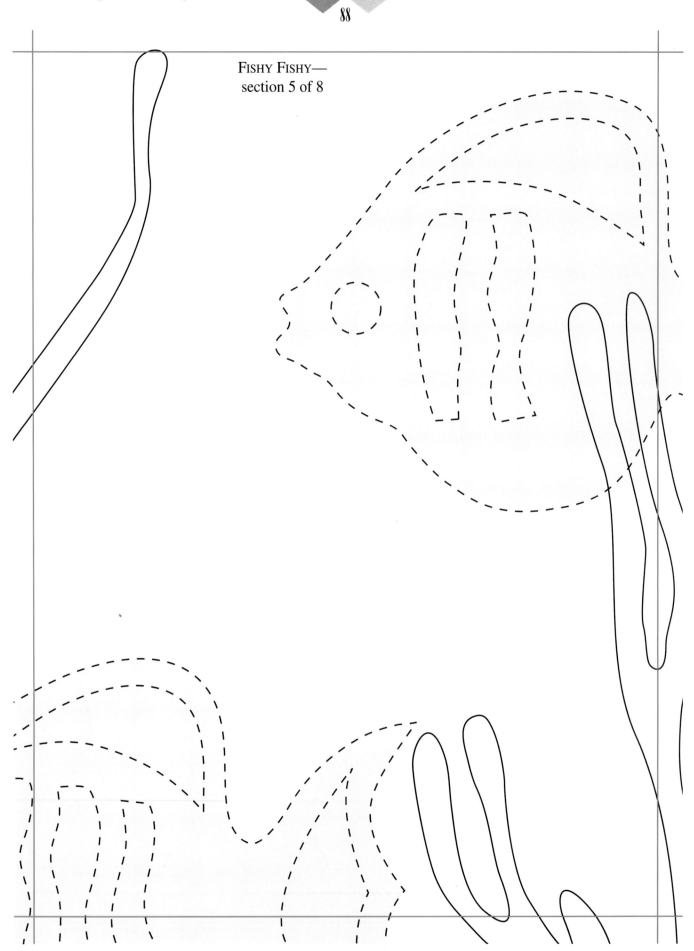

FISHY FISHY—
section 5 of 8

FISHY FISHY—
section 6 of 8

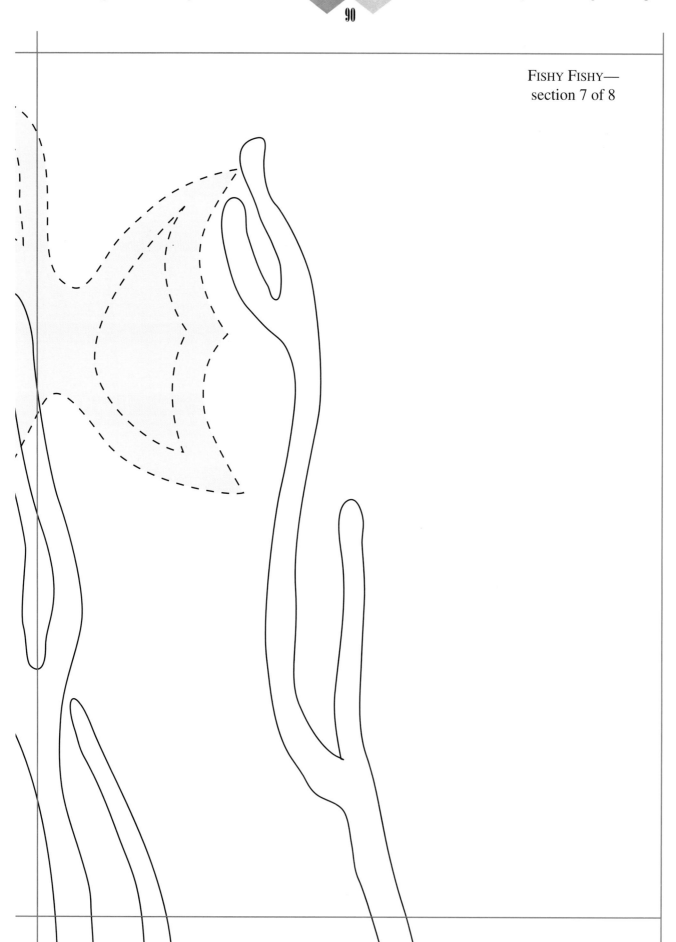

FISHY FISHY—
section 8 of 8

Tools and Supplies

Here are the basic tools and supplies you should have in your quilting pantry:

Rotary cutter

Be sure to change your blade frequently. A sharp blade will help you make accurate cuts, and it will cut through layers of stacked fat quarters.

Rotary-cutting mat

We suggest a minimum mat size of 17" x 23". Your fat quarters will fit on this size, and it is the most useful size for all your quilting projects. This is also the best size for taking to classes. You may like a larger one for home use. Smaller mats are available and they are useful for cutting around templates.

Rulers

The first ruler quilters should have is a 6" x 24" with clearly marked 1/8" increments. A 6" or 61/2" ruler is helpful for cutting smaller units from strips of fabric. Large square rulers (12" or more) are useful for squaring up blocks. Many rulers now have non-slip properties, making it easier to cut accurately.

Scissors

The pieces for these quilts can all be cut with a rotary cutter. A small pair of embroidery scissors is useful for snipping threads. Scissors for cutting paper and plastics are useful to have in your studio, too.

Sewing machine

There is a vast array of sewing machines available to us but a basic sewing machine is all that is needed for these quilts. A 1/4" patchwork foot for accurate piecing and a walking foot for machine quilting are invaluable. Your machine will function best if it is well tuned. Learn how to do basic cleaning and oiling and take your machine for a checkup once each year.

Sewing machine needles

For basic patchwork, we recommend a jeans/denim needle (80/12). Metafil or metallic needles work best with rayon threads. Topstitch needles (90/14) are useful for machine quilting with heavier threads. Check with your machine dealer for the brands they recommend for your sewing machine.

Thread

We use 100 percent cotton thread for piecing our quilts. We use a 50-weight thread in a range of neutral colors, such as cream, gray, beige, and tan. Use the darkest thread colors only when your fabrics are very dark.

For quilting, use hand-quilting thread when stitching by hand. There are many colors available to coordinate with any project. For machine quilting, we like invisible polyester, variegated cotton, rayon, or polyester threads. Be sure to use the needle size recommended for your thread choice.

Hand-sewing needles

You will need quilting betweens for hand quilting. You will also need a thimble for hand sewing. Try several types until you find the one that you find most comfortable to wear and use. If you cannot get used to a thimble, you may want to try some of the cushion pad products that are available to protect your fingers when sewing.

Pins

Use fine, sharp straight pins to accurately match seams when piecing. We like the ones with glass heads. For pin basting, use medium-sized non-rusting safety pins that have been designed for quilters. Some of you may prefer to spray baste your quilts. If you do, we recommend washing your project when it is completed to remove the spray basting product.

Fabric markers

If you use markers for quilting lines, be sure to follow the manufacturer's instructions for removing the marks.

Iron and ironing board

A steam iron and well-protected ironing surface will give the best results. Clean your iron regularly, following the instructions in the manual. This will greatly increase the longevity of your iron.

Template plastic

We prefer the gridded template plastic marked in 1/8" increments. It is transparent so you can trace patterns accurately. We use paper scissors for cutting our traced shapes.

Batting

Your quilt finishing technique, size of the project, and its intended use can help determine the type of batting you use. Polyester battings are lightweight and easy to quilt. They will stand up well to repeated washing.

Cotton-blend batting (80 percent cotton and 20 percent polyester) is our personal choice. We like the medium weight and the way it drapes. It is easy to quilt either by hand or by machine. It is also easy to care for and it washes well.

Resources

Susan Purney Mark and Daphne Greig
Patchworks Studio
2552 Eastdowne Road
Victoria, BC V8R 5P9
Canada

Susan and Daphne are available for
teaching and lecturing engagements.
Telephone: 250-595-4411 ■ Fax: 250-595-4377
E-mail Daphne: agreig@patchworkstudio.com
E-mail Susan: patchworkstudio@shaw.ca
Web site: www.patchworkstudio.com

Bali Fabrics, Inc., Princess Mirah Designs
21787 Eighth St. East Suite #1
Sonoma, California 95476
Telephone: 800-783-4612 ■ Fax: 707-996-9117
E-mail: info@balifab.com
Web site: www.balifab.com

Blank Quilting
65 West 36th Street
New York, NY 10018
Telephone: 888-442-5265 ■ Fax: 212-563-4733
E-mail: rburdette@blanktextiles.com
Web site: www.blanktextiles.com

Camelot Cottons
A division of Eugene Textiles, Inc.
9600 St. Laurent Blvd.
Suite #602
Montreal, Quebec H2N 1R2
Canada
Web site: www.camelotcottons.com

Susan Purney Mark

Susan's quilting journey began almost 30 years ago and has continued unabated, with enthusiasm building over the years. Quilts of all shapes, sizes, and colors have poured out of her studio, yet the stash of fabric continues to grow! Her interests include quilting history, design, and techniques, and she has recently begun to work with surface design, dyeing, painting, and embellishments. She also writes for several quilt magazines and teaches online at Quilt University. She has exhibited in Canada and the United States, and she is available to teach for quilt guilds, shops, and conferences.

In 1996 she formed a quilt pattern company, Patchworks Studio (www.patchworkstudio.com) with Daphne Greig. They have created dozens of patterns, online quilt series, and have coauthored two books, *Quilted Havens* and *Fat Quarter Frenzy,* with AQS. They continue to collaborate on many of their designs and publishing work.

Susan lives in Victoria, British Columbia, with her husband, Henry, where they enjoy gardening, hiking, and camping.

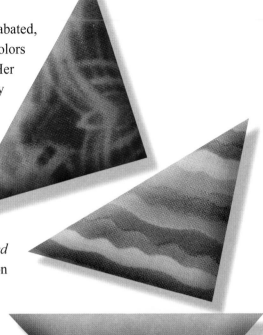

Daphne Greig

Daphne began sewing as a young girl, making outfits for her dolls. Her first teacher was her mother, an experienced sewer and embroiderer. She continued sewing garments until she discovered quilting in 1984. She began teaching quiltmaking at local quilt shops in 1990. Her work has been exhibited in Canada and the United States and she now travels internationally presenting innovative and entertaining lectures and workshops.

Daphne designs and maintains Patchworks Studio's very active Web site, including annual online series quilts. She regularly writes articles for several quilting magazines and teaches online at Quilt University.

Daphne continually expands her quilting and fiber art skills by attending workshops and experimenting with new techniques in her home studio in North Saanich, British Columbia.

Other AQS Books

This is only a small selection of the books available from the American Quilter's Society. AQS books are known worldwide for timely topics, clear writing, beautiful color photos, and accurate illustrations and patterns. The following books are available from your local bookseller, quilt shop, or public library.

Fat Quarter FRENZY — Susan Purney-Mark, Daphne Greig	WONDERFUL 1 Fabric Quilts — Kay Nickols	Celtic PIECED ILLUSIONS — KAREN COMBS
#6673　US$21.95	#7487　US$19.95	#7014　US$24.95
FABRIC Fandango — Combining Hand-Dyed and Commercial Prints — Gail Simpson	QUILTS for Ice Cream Lovers — Janet Jones Worley	BLENDED QUILT BACKGROUNDS — JEAN BIDDICK
#7490　US$22.95	#7075　US$21.95	#7078　US$24.95
MYSTERY QUILTS — RITA FISHEL	QUILTED ONE BLOCK MARVELS — CAROLYN SULLIVAN	NINE-PATCH Extravaganza — JUDY L. LAQUIDARA
#7079　US$22.95	#7491　US$22.95	#7484　US$22.95

Look for these books nationally.
Call or **Visit** our Web site at

1-800-626-5420
www.AmericanQuilter.com